MW01257957

Breaking Eve's Curse

by

Dr. Frank Hultgren

Copyright © 2004 by Dr. Frank Hultgren

Breaking Eve's Curse
by Dr. Frank Hultgren

Printed in the United States of America

ISBN 1-594678-99-5

All rights reserved solely by the author. The author guarantees all contents are original and do not infringe upon the legal rights of any other person or work. No part of this book may be reproduced in any form without the permission of the author. The views expressed in this book are not necessarily those of the publisher.

Unless otherwise indicated, Bible quotations are taken from the New King James Version. Copyright © 1996 by Broadman and Holman Publishers.

www.xulonpress.com

Acknowledgements

I like reading how authors thank all the people who help with the production of their books. While not knowing the author or the ones mentioned, a lot of work is put into the production of a manuscript of any size.

This book has been fifty years in coming to birth. I never thought I would be bold enough to produce such a document. I taught this in my meetings around the world and saw God do wonders.

President Richard Roberts of Oral Roberts University, and ORU First Lady, Lindsay, asked me to speak at a ladies' meeting and I gave this message. God poured out His Spirit and hundreds of ladies came for prayer and healing. At a later date I was asked to address the University with this message. It was as though the message was released for all to enjoy.

Many thanks to the Word Processing Department at ORU who worked so hard to bring this work to print. Also to Karen Sanders, who made the arrangements to print the book. Finally, thank you to the many others who were part of the process.

I am thrilled to have a very understanding wife, who has stood with me and helped in many ways to see this book and ministry come to pass.

Thank you, my darling wife June, for being more than a help-meet, but also a wife, mother to our four children, grandmother, advisor, counselor, and friend. Thank you. I love you, Honey.

Bless you all as you are healed.

Frank

Foreword

I have great confidence in the Word of God that what the Holy Spirit had men and women write in the sacred pages of the Bible is there for us to use so that we can come forth in the image of the Lord Jesus Christ.

We often forget that not only are we to be spiritual, but running parallel with the dreams, visions, and prophecy is also the ministry of the Holy Spirit to help us live normal, healthy lives. The Bible is very practical and admonishes us that while in this present world we have a textbook of how to live successfully.

The burning desire of my heart is to see people with needs having those problems answered and changed. I spent years in depression while building a successful church. The inward conflicts were often unbearable. Just as Jesus is touched with the feelings of our infirmities, we need also to recognize the hurts, sickness, and setbacks of all types. We need to procure through the Word and Holy Spirit the release Jesus promised us when He said "The Spirit of the Lord is upon me to open prison doors . . . of pain and disease. There is hope.

My next desire is to ask: Why have these issues not been dealt with before? Why are there not more healing ministers who focus on the real issues of women's health???

I bless you as you read. Be healed in Jesus' Name. Glory to God.

Contents

Introduction

I can remember quite clearly as a young boy, standing in the hallway of our home as my four sisters came in our front door with
my mother shaking and crying. They were all in their nightgowns,
and I couldn't work out what was happening, as all of these five
women were in a distressed state. I was about eight years of age,
and I did not know or understand anything that was happening. This
was 3 o'clock in the morning. The noise had awakened me, and I
had gone out into the hallway to see what the problem was. I was
hastily sent off to bed, but I never forgot the scene.

When I grew older, of course, I was told what the difficulty was.
My mother was going through the change of life. And the traumatic
experience she was suffering—a hormonal, emotional disturbance—had caused her to go running down the middle of the street
in the middle of the night, in the middle of a traumatic experience
that was beyond her control.

Years later, when I learned some of the medical understandings
of these situations, I was praying about all of this. I was in my first
church as a young man, twenty-two years of age, and praying that
the Lord would help me to help all the mothers who were suffering
like my mother.

My mother has since passed away, and I did not fully understand, even at that stage, everything that was happening in the
biological realm that women have as a daily companion. I remember
my mother because of the age in which we lived, which was some

fifty years ago; we didn't have the advantage of the technological advancement that we have today. Today they would have simply given my mother a hysterectomy, but they didn't have that advancement back then.

As a matter of fact, before I was born my mother was diagnosed with having a goiter, something that is seldom heard of today. She had to undergo an operation to remove it from under her chin because it was quite large, and she was six months pregnant with me. The doctor said, "We will either lose the mother or the baby. The mother is more important. If the baby is lost, well then, the mother is the one who needs to be saved." But, of course, the Lord intervened, and not only was the mother saved, but the baby was too.

My mother suffered, I guess like every other mother of that generation suffered. And because of a problem that was then known as a fallen womb, she hemorrhaged all the time and wore a diaper every day of her life because she hemorrhaged constantly. There was no known cure for it. I remember her saying to me one day, "When I get to heaven, I'm going to get my hands around Eve's scrawny neck, and I'm going to shake her until her teeth rattle!" Well, I guess she'll have to get in line, because there will be a lot of women who will be wanting to get hold of Eve's scrawny neck and give it the shaking that all of the women on the face of the earth would like to give her.

My mother was a wonderful lady. She had eight children—four boys, four girls—and was a very godly lady. She'd wake up at five o'clock in the morning, and to save electricity, she would light a candle and read her Bible and pray until the first one of us had to get up and go to work. Then she would make lunches for all the children who went to work and then those who were going to school. Then she would do all the washing and ironing for our big household.

My father's parents stayed with us, so we were a household-and-a-half. Then on top of that, as finances became harder, my mother went to work. She would do people's laundry, clean their houses, and then come home. In those days, it paid pitiful money. Today we would never do that kind of work for that amount of money. But that was the day's work. To her, it was necessary to have enough food to buy something to eat. And yet, she would still get up early, wait on the Lord, read her Bible, pray for our family, pray for missions, and then feed the horde of people who were in the house, do the washing and ironing, prepare the meals, and then go out to work.

What a devoted, uncomplaining, wonderful mother I had! She instituted a missions program in our church that is still continuing today. She just loved missions, and she loved the Lord. She wanted to see people saved, and particularly her family. Most of my brothers and sisters have found the Lord. Some are still on the edge, but we're all grateful for having a wonderful mother.

My father was one of those guys who would let my mother do all the work. They had a terrible relationship. He wouldn't work until all the children were self-supporting, then he worked. So our whole background was one of poverty. We grew in poverty, we saw poverty, we ate it, drank it, and slept it. We had two children in a bed and four people in a room.

I remember when I started to go to Bible college. I would get out of bed and go to the college. Then I'd come home, and my uncle would get out of my bed to go work the night shift, while I got in and slept during the night. The bed was never cold.

We had a negative upbringing, except that my mother would teach us about God. She would demand that on Sundays we went to church and Sunday school, which we did all the time. I, personally, went to Sunday school from the age of six, and went through all the grades and all the classes that there were in Sunday school at that time. I went into the young adults' Bible class, and from there I went to Bible school, then into the ministry. As of May 2002, I have been in the ministry fifty years without a break. But my mother laid the foundation—my sick mother, my poor, poor mother who suffered all those things.

One day in my first church, while I was praying and considering all that my mother had suffered and gone through, it was as though the Lord spoke to me. He said, "My son, there is healing for women in the Cross." I don't know that I had ever heard the voice of the Lord before, or had ever received a word from the Lord like that before, but I walked around in a daze for days. I couldn't believe

God had spoken to me, and why would He tell me that there is healing for women? I was too young to start proclaiming this, although from that time on, I have had a desire to see women healed.

Down through the years, I have prayed for women. I've made altar calls for women from Papua, New Guinea, to Australia, to America, and to Malaysia. Everywhere I go as the Lord leads, I pray for women. I love having ladies' meetings, because I feel that there is healing for women in the Cross of Jesus Christ.

What the Lord told me more than four decades ago I am seeing come to pass. I am writing this book so that women may be healed, made whole, and come to a place where they are accepted in the whole body of Christ for who they are. In Jesus' name, I believe there is healing for women!

CHAPTER ONE

The Lie of satan

This book may be a little controversial. There will be people who will find Scriptures that they can use against the doctrine of healing for women. But as I stated in the Introduction, the Lord says there is healing for women in the Atonement, and that means everything to do with women that has come as a result of the Fall.

We are going to look at some Scriptures very closely and endeavor to establish that there is a great neglect on this particular subject. As a matter of fact, I am quite surprised that there hasn't been a book written about this by doctors and men of God who have researched this to find out why women are dying, why they are sick, and why, at any sort of altar call, there are more women than men who come forward because they have diseases associated with their gender.

I would like to point out in this first chapter just how satan has a bearing on all of our thinking and how he has programmed man not to accept woman in her rightful role. Woman has a rightful role, created by God in the beginning for specific tasks. Satan has seen to it that woman's tasks are now clouded because of his lying, and men everywhere have chosen to accept his lies rather than look at the truth. There are commentators, preachers, and writers who say that women are to be satisfied, that sickness is to be part of their role because of Eve's sin in the Garden of Eden at the beginning.

I want to point out that satan is a liar. Jesus said to the Jewish leaders in John 8:44, <u>NKJV</u>, *You are of your father the devil, and the desires of your father you want to do. He was a murderer from the beginning, and does not stand in the truth, because there is no truth in him. When he speaks a lie, he speaks from his own resources, for he is a liar and the father of it.*

Every ungodly person is influenced with a satanic nature. They have imbibed—taken into themselves—the lies of satan. They do not know the truth. They cannot walk in the truth, nor in the light, because the light and the truth are not in them. They have a nature that is not of God. It is a fallen nature; therefore, satan has access to their minds to program their minds.

This is in II Corinthians 4:4. It says that the god of this world has blinded the minds of them who do not believe, so that they cannot believe the Gospel. So already, before we discuss any matter whatsoever, they have a bias toward that which is not truth. So we need to renew our minds and reprogram our lifestyles to accept the truth of the Lord Jesus Christ—His life, His covenants, and everything that He has for us.

Jesus' description of satan is that he is a liar and the father of lies. Is it any wonder that when Adam and Eve were tempted in Genesis 3, <u>NKJV</u>, that satan spoke to them along this line and said, *God knows that in the day you eat of it* [the fruit of the tree in the midst of the garden] *your eyes will be opened and you will be like God, knowing good and evil. So when the woman saw that the tree was good for food, that it was pleasant to the eyes, and a tree desirable to make one wise, she took of its fruit and ate (vv. 5, 6).* So Eve saw this by looking with her eyes—the lust of the eyes, the pride of life—and she was elevated in her thinking because of the satanic influence (see I John 2:16).

Let us not underestimate the power of this temptation. This was not just the enemy using the disguise of a serpent to beguile the woman. It was all satanic forces in operation. The deception, the lying, the desire for pleasure, the pride—appealing to her pride to be like God, to be like the God who used to walk through the Garden of Eden in the cool of the day, who would talk with her and fellowship with her and Adam—and here comes this satanic influence. It would have been apart from God's power, the greatest force on the face of the earth.

The overwhelming, drawing attraction that was leveled at Eve's soul so that she began to see and desire that which had never been kindled for this sort of thing before was started, ignited, and fanned by the persuasive, charismatic voice and influence of the master deceiver. He tricked her and deceived her into violating the commandments of the Lord. This is so great, so graphic! What Eve did is eternal, because she brought sin into the human race where there had been no sin. And it didn't come simply by a choice; she was deceived with the greatest deception that the master craftsman of deception could bring upon her. Please take into consideration how conniving, cheating, deceiving, and appealing to the senses that this old serpent, the devil, really was when he deceived this beautiful, wonderful man and his wife. Eve was deceived, and she sinned, violating the commandments of God.

Satan is a liar. He lies and has always lied. He doesn't know anything else but to distort the truth. This is why there are problems in churches and why there are problems in homes—because he lies. He amplifies things that are satanic. He takes the truth and twists it for his own ends, and half the time we do not know the truth.

We come into confusion because satan is a confuser, and he brings contention. Where there are any of these things, you can be sure that he is lurking somewhere in the shadows, because he delights in murder and shameful things. All the time he's trying to debilitate the human race so that it will not reflect the image of the Lord Jesus Christ, who is the truth, the God of all truth, and the Spirit of truth. The Godhead, who is truth, is constantly opposed by the enemy. Satan is constantly defrauding and cheating men and women out of their guarantee of life eternal and the abundant goodness that God has for the human race.

Satan is in opposition to all the affairs of man. By nature, he is a liar. In everything he does, he lies. He takes away hope, he takes away joy, he takes away pleasure, and in their place he brings sickness, pain, disease, and the things that will destroy and divide to make man like himself. There is no truth in him. He cannot speak the truth, and he hates those who love the truth.

The serpent knows no rules. He attempted to deceive Jesus

Christ during the Temptation. He tempts every Christian somewhere along the line. The devil walks around like a roaring lion seeking whom he may devour (see I Peter 5:8). He never gives up. He is determined, even though he knows his time is short. He is absolutely determined to bring conflict between leaders, to bring division in churches, and to bring sickness and shame upon everybody. He wants to ruin the potential of life and power that God has invested in every human heart.

Every person on the face of the earth has the potential and the ability to fulfill the Word of God. Yet the lies and the deception of the enemy violate the commandments and the prophetic flow of the Spirit, to bring us down, to bring us to poverty, to bring us to a crust of bread. The pain and suffering that is in the human race is the result of how satan has dealt with us. He has done his job very, very well.

So, on the subject that we are talking about today—the ministry that the Holy Spirit wants women to have to bless them—satan has targeted so that they will not rise to be the reflection of the Godhead. We will deal with these things in another chapter.

CHAPTER TWO

The Curse of Eve

Would you say, as a general statement, that there is healing for women? When it comes to the great message of the atonement, salvation, and the fact that there is a covenant that God made with the human race—does the covenant and salvation and healing deal with the *whole* human race? Is there a separate ministry for women as opposed to men? Is there a new covenant?

Why is it that women have breast cancer, hysterectomies, and all the other diseases and problems that women have that men don't have? We know that women are made differently. They have a different role. Scientists tell us that even the hair structures of men and women are different. Their blood is different. Their skin is different. Their make-up is different. Men and women are different—not necessarily one better than the other—but different. And because the woman is able to reproduce life—her body is made to reproduce life—she has motherly instincts that are absolutely devoid in men. And so, there is a breakdown in human life because of this, because the enemy comes in like a flood to bring discouragement and to bring pain, and I believe it's a lie.

Let us look at the Scriptures to see if there is a curse upon woman. Does God put a curse upon women—Eve's curse? As I said in the introduction, my mother blames Eve, and rightly so. Does Eve carry the results of that sin right through to today? Is she forgiven? Is she in heaven? Does she still take the blame? And what has God done about it? Has He repaired the breach? And is there provision now for women who come to Christ? Can they be healed? Or do they have to still carry the shame of Eve's past?

I want you to turn with me to the Bible, and let's see what the Word of God has to say about this in Genesis 3, <u>NKJV</u>: *And the Lord God said to the woman, What is this you have done? And the woman said, The serpent deceived me, and I ate.* Now notice carefully what God said to the serpent: *Because you have done this, you are cursed more than all cattle, and more than every beast of the field; on your belly you shall go, and you shall eat dust* [that is, flesh, because the flesh goes to dust] *all the days of your life. And I will put enmity between you and the woman, and between your seed and her Seed; He shall bruise your head, and you shall bruise His heel* (vv. 13, 14).

In these verses, we find that God curses the serpent. He said, "You are cursed." I don't know whether the serpent was on legs, but the Bible says that the serpent will crawl on his belly, but the work of the serpent is to come after dust. He eats dust, or flesh. This is why the enemy is able to appeal to our flesh—to our senses, our sensitivity, our emotions. The works of the flesh and the lusts of the eyes and the nature of sin that is in us at birth—if we don't yield and commit ourselves to the Lord, if we don't allow God to deal with all of these things, then satan has access to us. He has the ability to tempt us, to draw aside our hearts from right, and to deceive us again, because he eats flesh. He comes after the uncrucified life, the undedicated life, the undedicated mind.

But the curse is upon satan more than upon all cattle and every beast of the field. It is interesting that verse 15 says: *I will put enmity between you and the woman, and between your seed and her Seed.* We know already that "her Seed" was the Lord Jesus Christ, but "your seed," speaking of the serpent, means that in every generation there would be a demonic influence against woman. And this is why, in history, we find that woman has been put down.

It is only in the last few years that woman has been able to attain her rightful place in the human race. The women's liberation movement was seen as being opposed to men simply because woman was trying to get and take her rightful place. Because of this, there are very strong women, and some of them are matriarchal types that rose because of the Fall, and of course, put the man down to bring the woman up. Out of all this bitterness and confusion there was deception. But it was the voice of woman crying out to take her place, which many men did not like. Of course, those women who never had a problem in their lives and were balanced in their experience were not worried about it, and they knew that, generally, the women's lib movement was anti-God and spawned by the enemy anyway.

But the first part of verse 15 is the interesting part: *I will put enmity between you and the woman.* From that day to this, there has been enmity against the woman. Satan hates women. This is why women are more easily deceived than men, because of their sensitivity. God has built into them emotion so that they can sense and feel. They have motherhood qualities and gentleness that is reminiscent of true women of God. They have a desire all the time for right, for increasing knowledge, for wisdom and understanding, and to know the reason why. All of these are the qualities that God has put in woman; therefore, in many, many ways women have another side of intelligence and wisdom that men lack.

Women are a special handiwork of God and are no less than men. Their bodies are more unique than men's. Their minds and hearts think differently because God has made them to be different, to add variety and to bring balance to man. This is why woman was made. God said to Adam that he wasn't complete without a helpmeet, and He made the helpmeet, Eve. They were a composite pair, but they became one—one in mind, one in motive, one in purpose, and one in their desire to please God. So when Eve fell, she brought the curse upon Adam, but Adam wasn't deceived; he transgressed and sinned.

There has been enmity between the woman and satan from that day to this. A lot of the health problems that women have and the fact that they have been put down and hated by many nations is because of this enmity. Satan hates women. He hates everything about them. This is why he will push them to the extreme. I believe this is why some women sell their bodies in prostitution—because he hates them. It's all a satanic ploy to bring woman down and debilitate her so that she will be despised in the human race.

Many cultures demand that women cover their bodies completely. You never see their faces. They never go out in public without being totally veiled. But in Bible days, the women that were veiled were harlots or prostitutes. It is not really the will of God for women to have their faces veiled. Second Corinthians 3:18 tells us that with unveiled face, we behold the glory of the Lord. The Lord is looking for openness. He wants us to be confident, full of faith, full of the Word, and to be beautiful people in His presence. In no way is woman to be put down.

History brings out this shocking treatment of women down through the years. Most nations have a very poor record of what they have done to their womenfolk. Even today, in some countries, as a fellow gets a little bit older and he feels the desire to have a younger wife, he can go pick another wife. It's because in some cultures women are for men's sexual pleasure. The older women can use the younger ones as servants, but the women are just like toys for the men. And this shame that has come upon the human race is because the few verses in Genesis have been totally misunderstood and totally misrepresented. I want to show you how the enemy has continually harassed women and lied, saying they were a second-class part of the kingdom of God.

In Genesis 3:16, NKJV, we see a most interesting thing. To the woman God said, *I will greatly multiply your sorrow and your conception; in pain you shall bring forth children; your desire shall be for your husband, and he shall rule over you.* This is one verse that God gave to Eve, and if you look at it carefully, you will see that there was no curse upon Eve. No curse. Eve was not cursed. So how did we get the interpretation down through the centuries that woman is cursed? I wonder how many people reading this book believe the woman is cursed. But the Bible never ever says she is cursed!

The Bible does tell us that there would be anger from satan against the woman because she produced the Lord Jesus Christ. There was a young lady who remained clean, pure, and was a virgin, and God was able to use her to bring forth the Lord Jesus Christ. But all through the generations women have been hated and despised, and they attribute it to Genesis 3:16. Yet this Scripture never ever says that the woman is cursed. Woman is not cursed.

I want to break Eve's curse today because it's a lie from the devil. He has brought that lie into minds, particularly the minds of men. It has also infiltrated the minds of little girls and stays there until they are grandmothers. Women tell the younger generation coming up that they are beneath men, and that they have all their feminine problems as a part of Eve's curse.

I want you to look at Genesis 3:16, <u>NKJV,</u> again and show me what the curse was, because there was no curse, but judgment. God says, *I will greatly multiply your sorrow and your conception; in pain you shall bring forth children.* Concerning the body, show me where there is a curse. There is no curse, but there is a judgment. So when it comes time to give birth to a baby, a woman has sorrow and much pain. But what about all the other sicknesses and diseases that go along with human life? God's Word never says that women shall suffer PMT—premenstrual tension. It never says that women shall have hysterectomies. It never says anything about hemorrhaging. It never says anything about all the problems associated with woman-hood, such as the change of life—the biological change in their lifestyle. It never says anything about that. It only talks about conception and bringing forth children.

I believe that the deception of the enemy is that during all of their lives, women think they have to have cramps, pain, and all the problems that go along with womanhood, until they are old. Then they lose calcium out of their bones, and diseases wrack their bodies. The Bible does not say that, and I'm looking for it as I write these words. I'm reading my Bible to try to find where it says that woman's body is to be the <u>battleground of health.</u> According to <u>verse 16,</u> single women would never have any problems with their bodies; only those who were married, and then only those who were going to have children. If you don't have children, there's no conception. If there's no conception, you don't have a baby. And so it means that all the women who have babies are judged, and all the women who don't have babies are not judged.

The deception of satan is that *all* women have been cursed by God, and their punishment is that they will have all of these physical problems until the day they die, including menstruation, menopause, hysterectomies, cancer, tumors, cysts, fibroids, growths, adhesions, and hemorrhaging. But that is just not in the Bible. This is the deception of the enemy.

If that's the case, what about Adam? To Adam God said, *Because you have heeded the voice of your wife, and have eaten from the tree of which I commanded you, saying, 'You shall not eat of it': cursed is the ground for your sake; in toil you shall eat of it all the days of your life. Both thorns and thistles it shall bring forth for you, and you shall eat the herb of the field. In the sweat of your face you shall eat bread till you return to the ground, for out of it you were taken; for dust you are, and to dust you shall return (vv. 17-19).*

So there is one verse for Eve and three verses for Adam. And what God says to Adam is that the curse is on the ground. It doesn't say that Adam was cursed. It says, *In the sweat of your face you shall eat bread till you return to the ground.* It doesn't say that Adam would be sick. It doesn't say that he would have all sorts of problems because of the sin he committed. It never says anywhere in these verses that the judgment of God was on him. But two things were cursed: the serpent was cursed, and so was the ground. But Adam and Eve were judged. The judgment of God was upon them. For Eve there would be difficulty in conception and pain in childbearing. Adam's body was not mentioned. It says the ground was cursed and he would have to plow the ground by the sweat of his face. This is why men perspire on their faces. The perspiring face speaks of work, it speaks of the flesh, and it speaks of the judgment of God. The next time you see a man sweating, you can say it's the result of Adam's judgment. The next time a woman giving birth to a baby cries out, you can say that's the result of God's judgment. However, the Bible doesn't say anything about prenatal trauma, postnatal trauma, and all the difficulties that the body experiences. The body is not cursed. Women experience difficulty in birth, and man has the sweating of the face, but there is no curse upon either of them.

Now this should clear the way for us to start to believe that God has an answer for us concerning healing, health, and blessing. III John 2 says He wants us to be in health, and He wants us to prosper even as our soul prospers. God is not going to destroy our bodies. Second Corinthians 6:19 clearly and distinctly says that the body is the temple of the Holy Spirit. So in the original Creation, God created Adam and Eve. He judged them for their sin. He did not send sickness upon their bodies. He sent judgment. He put the curse upon satan and upon the earth. You have to get an understanding of this in your mind and in your spirit. You have to start to recognize that what you have believed in the past about the curse of Eve is a lie—satan's lie, satan's deception to let us think that sickness is the judgment of God because of Eve's sin.

I want to break Eve's curse. Let's believe that the lie of the curse of Eve is broken off our mind, taken out of our mentality, and straightaway we can start to see the healing blessing of God in our lives when we come out from under that deception. The deception is that we think we're deceived. But we are not deceived. We are of the truth and we are walking in truth, and we are not going to believe the lie of the enemy! This understanding should be liberating to women all over the world—to realize that they do not have to be under the iron heel of a lie that satan has rubbed into our spirits and into our minds, making us captives of the falsehood of the curse of Eve.

Let me state it plainly for you again. God never cursed Eve. God never cursed Adam. You do not have anything upon you that is the result of Eve's sin, except that there is still pain in childbirth.

So once we have that cleared up, we're going to look at our bodies and see the problems that are there, and say, "Where did all these things come from?" Well, it's because of satan's deception and the enmity that is in his heart against woman because she was chosen to bear the Savior, the Lord Jesus Christ. I want you to lay your hands on your body and rebuke that deception. Lay your hands on your mind, and say, "I am not going to be deceived by the enemy anymore. I am free from the curse of the original sin. I am not under it. It is a lie. Jesus Christ has come to set me free from the curse of the law and the curse that satan has put on us. God never cursed me. I have never been cursed by God. I am free from every curse. The curse is on the Cross, but there is no curse on my life because of Eve's sin. I break the curse of Eve's sin, in Jesus' Name. Right now, I begin to receive healing because of the atonement of Jesus Christ. I believe that there is healing for women through the Cross of Christ. And I thank You, Lord Jesus, for liberating me from this lie, in Jesus' Name."

CHAPTER THREE

Breaking the Power of Transgressions

I want to continue our discussion on Eve and how she was able to come out from under the judgment of God. First Timothy 2:13-15, <u>NKJV,</u> are controversial verses regarding this subject. Verse 13, *For Adam was formed first, then Eve. And Adam was not deceived, but the woman being deceived, fell into transgression.* Now her sin was first the deception, and secondly, the transgression.

In the previous chapter we talked about Eve, that the judgment of God would be sorrow in conception and pain in birth. That is Old Testament. That was what God said in the first few chapters of Genesis, but here it comes to the New Testament side of the Cross of Calvary. And even though in verse 14 it says woman was deceived and the woman fell into transgression, verse 15 says, *Nevertheless she will be saved in childbearing if they continue in faith, love, and holiness, with self-control.*

Isn't it remarkable that New Testament scholars have never discovered this verse that says the original judgment of God upon woman has now been taken away, that because of the Cross of Jesus Christ, there doesn't have to be the trauma of childbirth? It is taken away. The many sorrows and the many pains associated with a woman's life because of her womanliness —because of her cycles of life—the Bible says that now there is love, and there is peace. There is faith. There is holiness.

To have children is a wonderful blessing and there is nothing wrong with it, but fear of childbirth causes many women to have all sorts of difficulties, and it is because we have given in to satan's lie that tells us a woman's body is to be the playground of pain and sorrow because of Eve's transgression. Yet the Bible clearly says that woman shall be saved in childbirth.

"Saved" means health, blessing, the breaking of the curse, the blessing of God upon the reproductive parts of a woman's body. I think this is absolutely fantastic. If I were a woman and had never read these verses, I would be absolutely astounded to think that I had been under the lie of the devil for years and had put up with all sorts of embarrassing situations in my body because I was a woman, and I did not have to do it. The Bible says, *Nevertheless, she will be saved in childbearing.*

And again, I want to point out the fact that the Scripture doesn't talk about single women or people who don't have children. According to Genesis, there is no judgment upon single women or childless women—only those having babies. All that original judgment is eradicated because of the Cross of Calvary, and a woman can enter into peace and health and life because she is going to be saved from the judgment of God that was upon Eve, when it comes to womanly areas. Yes, women need to press in and break the lies that doctors, philosophers, scientists, and hard-hearted, ungodly people have put upon them.

You may not be aware of this, but when chloroform was first discovered some years ago, the clergy cried out against the man who discovered it and said, "What have you done? You cannot give chloroform to a woman having a baby. She has to have pain because that's what the Bible says." And they outlawed chloroform being given to women in childbirth because they believed it was violating the Scripture. It was not violating the Scripture. Hard-hearted, deceived men have put down and degraded women and made them suffer because of their own self-righteousness and misinterpretation of the Scripture, because the Word says that she shall be saved. That is black and white. It is clear that woman can be saved from pain in childbirth. If it is through the modern technology we have today or through old-fashioned chloroform, who cares? God wants women to be in health and to prosper as well as any other person on the face of the earth.

First Timothy 2:14 is interesting. It says that the woman was deceived and fell into transgression. Come with me to the real chapter of conversion and salvation in Isaiah 53. What a marvelous section of scripture this is! It explains how our wonderful Lord Jesus took our sins and sicknesses and made a way of salvation and redemption for us. What a wonderful Savior He is! As we have faith in Him, faith in what He has done, as Timothy says, women will be saved in childbirth through faith, love, and holiness. So through faith in what God has done, faith in His provision, and faith in His Word, our bodies are being continually brought into the image of Christ.

Isaiah 53:3, <u>NKJV,</u> says, *He [Jesus] is despised and rejected by men.* Not only is Jesus despised and rejected by men, but women are despised and rejected by men. And one of the chief problems women have is that they carry a sense of being despised. Often despised by their own gender, but certainly despised by some men in the workplace, where men poke fun at women, ridicule them, and think of them as sex objects. Because of this, women think they are despised.

Women are often rejected when it comes to filling executive positions or being ministers of the Gospel. Some pastors put down women, will not allow them into their pulpits, and despise women's ministries. I think it is absolutely diabolical to think that some of the great gifts women have are not heard, and they are not able to express their thoughts or their God-given ideas because of the bigotry of ecclesiastical men who want to make room for men and put down women. I believe as Jesus told me, that there is healing for women in the Cross. And Jesus bore the rejection that women suffer, because Jesus is the Savior and Lord of our life.

When it comes to the ministry gifts—the apostle, prophet, teacher, evangelist, pastor—just in recent years have we allowed women into pulpits and recognized that God could put a gift in them, that they can pastor or shepherd people. And teachers—I have heard some fine, wonderful lady teachers. And evangelists—well, they have an ability to minister to the lost and get them saved. And prophetesses—we have seen them in this nation and in many other places, but they really have to struggle for recognition because they are women.

I have hardly ever heard anybody say that a woman can be an apostle. Very, very few men will ever recognize that. But I have met some women whom I believe have an apostolic gift. They are pastors of churches—churches larger than some led by men—and they have an outreach, a giving, a place in society, and are recognized in society because of their giftings.

The funny part about the whole thing is that the gift of the Lord Jesus Christ is not feminine, nor is it masculine; it comes from Christ. And when it comes to the gifts of the Spirit, God's Word never says anywhere that women cannot be used in the gifts of the Spirit. I have searched the Scriptures to find out if there is a male anointing or a female anointing, and there is no such beast.

The bigotry that we have in our hearts—the rejection of women in places of leadership—has caused us to squash many truths and revelations that women are able to bring us. The ministry gifts are not feminine. They are gifts of Christ.

The ministry is not masculine or feminine. It has nothing to do with gender, age, or race. It has to do with the grace of the Lord Jesus Christ. If God chooses to speak through Balaam's ass, or speak through a man, or speak through a woman, that is His choice (See Numbers 22:28-30). If He chooses to speak through a woman, so be it. It is not the woman's words. It is the Word of the Lord that we want to hear, and a woman will bring the insight that God intended for her to produce. We need to take the blinders off our eyes and ask the Lord to bring us insight. The god of this world, satan, has blinded our minds so that we cannot see the great revelation of the liberation of women into their rightful place in ministry and in life.

Women need to put their attitude of being despised and their feeling of being rejected on the Cross. You are not despised; you are purchased with the blood of Jesus Christ. There is no male or female in heaven. And you are a part of the body of Christ as a person, not because of your gender or race or age, but because Jesus loves you. You did not choose to be a woman. You never had any choice in the matter. You are what you are because that is what God wanted you to be. So come to the fullness of what He has for you.

Verse three of Isaiah 53 says that He is a man despised and rejected of men, a Man of sorrows and acquainted with grief. Isn't it interesting that on the Cross of Calvary, Jesus Christ took the judgment of Eve and He became a man of sorrows? The word "sorrows" in Hebrew is pains. He became a man of sorrows, and He was acquainted with grief or sickness. Verse 4, NKJV, says, *Surely He has borne our griefs* [that's our sicknesses] *and carried our sorrows* [which is, literally, our pains].

Again, what was the judgment of God upon Eve? It was sorrow and pain. What did Jesus bear on the Cross? Sorrow and pain. What was God's judgment upon woman? Sorrow and pain. What has Jesus delivered woman from? Sorrow and pain!

But that is not all that Isaiah 53, NKJV, says. As a matter of fact, a very interesting little section in verse 5 says, *He was wounded for our transgressions.* Eve transgressed. Timothy says that she was deceived and fell into transgression. Jesus, on the Cross, paid the price for her grief, her sorrow—which was her pain and her sicknesses. Everything to do with the woman's misadventure through being woman, He took to the Cross. And He was wounded for our transgressions. He was wounded for Eve's transgressions. That means they are forgiven.

The latter part of verse 8 says, *For the transgressions of My people He was stricken.* He was wounded and stricken for our transgressions. So part of Jesus' suffering on the Cross—the stripes he bore, the wounding He received—was to pay the price for all of Eve's transgressions so that the transgressions and the consequences were paid for by Jesus Christ's atoning death on Calvary. And it specifically uses the words that God used in the beginning, to take away from our hearts and our minds and to put satan to a disadvantage so that his deception would be broken, that we may enter into health and life, blessing and prosperity, because Jesus paid it all.

The latter part of verse 12 says, *He was numbered with the transgressors, and He bore the sin of many, and made intercession for the transgressors.* So if Eve had transgressed, He identified with Eve's sin and bore it in His body on the tree. He also made intercession. He cried out to God upon the Cross and said, *Father, forgive them for they do not know what they do* (Luke 23:34, NKJV).

Satan has to have a ground to work on to bring about a deception, and the ground he has worked on is that he has told women that they are cursed, that their feminine ailments are the judgment of God and they'll never be free from them. Because of this misrepresentation of truth, women have believed a lie. When it comes to verses like Isaiah 53:12, we do not appreciate what God has done for us in wiping out the sins of the past. He initiated a new race through Jesus Christ, and the old is finished by the power of the blood of Jesus Christ. All the handwriting of ordinances that was against us, and there were a lot of things against the human race—in Colossians 2:14 it says that they have been paid for in full, and now we have redemption from the curse, from the transgression, from the judgment, and we are free. And whom the Son sets free is free indeed!

The Amplified translation of 1 Timothy 2:15 is very interesting. It amplifies the childbearing aspect of womanhood, but it has a different slant on it. It says that a woman shall be saved *through the child-bearing, that is, by the birth of the [divine] Child.* This is eluding to Mary, the mother of Jesus, when she gave birth to the Lord Jesus Christ.

If Eve produced sin into the human race, Mary produced the Savior to conquer that sin from the human race. I can't imagine Mary, once the Holy Spirit overshadowed her and she conceived the Lord Jesus, having morning sickness the first three months, having cramps, vomiting, or any of the other excruciating things that can go along with the birth of a baby. Do you think she was bedridden for nine months? Did she have all sorts of pains in her tummy? Did she walk around holding her back, saying, "I've got a bad back"? And did she have to lie down because she was having headaches? I wonder if she had any hemorrhaging. Do you think she had a rugged time bearing this Baby who is the Savior of the world? I cannot imagine that!

Mary knew immediately when the Holy Spirit came upon her and she conceived by the Holy Spirit. And I imagine that it was with great joy that she noticed the changes in her body, the rounding of her breasts, and her tummy beginning to fill out. I believe she experienced great joy and, I would imagine, great anointings of the Holy Spirit. And not for one moment did she have the slightest bit of morning sickness or any other sickness, traumatic experience, or pain.

You see, it is my own considered opinion that with the birth of the Lord Jesus through Mary, womanhood was reinstated to the original place of honor and dignity that God gave Eve at the beginning. What Eve lost because of sin, Mary regained because of holiness. Not that Mary is our savior, but she, with Jesus Christ, was the beginning of a new race. In Adam all die; in Christ all are made alive. Mary reinstated the blessing upon woman—not eulogizing her or making her a saint above what is normally and rightfully hers—simply because she was a pure maiden, a virgin, a young lady who gave birth to the Lord Jesus Christ. I believe that when she had this Baby, all the things that happened with her and her life were normal, natural, beautiful, pure, and God-glorifying. I do not believe that with her pain—can you imagine her sweating and being traumatized and fainting as she was giving birth to the Savior of the world? I believe that the birth of the Lord Jesus Christ was a perfect birth. And even though Mary was a human vessel, she was a greatly anointed human vessel, and I believe that Christ's birth was the beginning of a new time for women.

The old time for women should have ended, but we haven't been taught this. We come under the old dispensation of Eve. Even though Eve was deceived and she transgressed, the Cross of Jesus Christ totally eliminated anything that came from the Fall that was in any way a curse.

In Jesus Christ we are new creatures and we are waiting for the redemption of our bodies. I believe the more we assimilate the truth of healing, the more we assimilate the truth of the creative nature of His redeeming grace, the holier we will become and the more like Christ our bodies will be. The sickness and diseases that have ravaged our lives will come to an end because this is our hour of healing and of the power of God.

We have yet to fully assimilate what Jesus did for us. We have yet to fully understand what Mary and the birth of the Lord Jesus Christ meant for women. It brought women back to where God intended them to be. Generally, unrighteous men go back to the Garden of Eden instead of going forward to the manger. We can go even further to the Cross where our sorrows, our pains, and our transgressions have all been paid for in full and where we have a redemption that redeems us from all the Old Testament curses, including hereditary sicknesses and diseases. There is power in the Cross and power in the blood. However, until we fully appreciate the power of the Cross of Christ—which is foolishness to them that perish, but to us who are saved it is the power of God—and we appropriate the power of the resurrection life of Christ, until we fully assimilate it, we will be badgered by the lion, the devil, who walks around seeking whom he may devour with his enmity, his viciousness, and his lies (see I Peter 5:8). We believe his lies rather than believing God's truth. It is easier to believe that we are sick, and we accept that it is just part of the human experience rather than believing that Jesus Christ died on the Cross to save us—body, soul, and spirit.

So, to me, this verse in I Timothy 2:15 in the Amplified version says it was through the Child-bearing and birth of the divine Child that women were liberated from the trauma of a judged womanhood.

CHAPTER FOUR

Menstrual Sickness

Do you think that Jesus Christ would violate the law that God had laid down? What if God has said to Eve in the Old Testament that because of her sin women would have physical diseases and, in particular, problems in reproduction? What right has the Son of God to interfere with His Father's will? Who has assigned this sickness to women? What right has the Son of God to move in and offer her divine healing? The legality of many will cause women to be suppressed and isolated from the healing power of God's love and grace. As a man, how am I to know just everything that happens in the woman's physical body during childbirth and menstruation? I have two daughters and my wife, and I have a very fine friend, a lady doctor, gynecologist, Dr. Margaret Smith, who specializes in ladies' health problems, particularly birth. She has delivered thousands of babies and performed many operations on women to help them with their female complaints. And now, in these latter years, she is specializing in menopause. She is a very interesting lady, a delightful person and very knowledgeable. Dr. Smith has written papers of her findings concerning these things to many doctors, seminars, and conventions in different parts of the world. And she has helped me with several of the things that I am going to discuss in this chapter.

Would Jesus have knowingly violated the Scriptures that God brought upon woman? If He knew that there was healing for women, did His healing ministry violate the commandments of God, or did He fulfill the Word of the Lord and come and heal women of all their diseases?

Matthew 9:20-22 says, *Behold, a woman, which was diseased with an issue of blood twelve years, came behind him, and touched the hem of His garment: for she said within herself, If I may but touch his garment, I shall be whole. But Jesus turned him about, and when he saw her, he said, 'Daughter, be of good comfort; thy faith hath made thee whole.' And the woman was made whole from that hour.* Isn't that remarkable? Here was a woman who had been hemorrhaging for twelve years from a disease. Mark 5:26 says that she had spent all of her finances trying to find healing. In those days they used all types of bizarre methods to try and stem the flow of this type of hemorrhaging.

Twelve years of hemorrhaging makes one very weak. Did anyone ever say that it was a curse? The Old Testament Scripture says that during the time of menstruation, a woman had to be apart from others so that there would be no embarrassment for her during that time (See Leviticus 15:19-30). But here was a woman who had suffered with this disease for twelve years, had gone to numerous physicians and was not made any better but was possibly worse; and, yet, she never thought she was in the wrong to come up to Jesus and touch the hem of His garment. And Jesus turned around to her and said, *Be of good comfort.* He never said, "Get away from Me; you are cursed." He never put her aside. He never put her down. He never berated her because, number one, she was female or, number two, because she had this disease. How humiliating it was for her and all of her friends to be conscious of this law and deal with the matter all the time! But she went to Jesus, and He comforted her. Jesus blessed her. Jesus loved her. And Jesus healed her. Remarkable, isn't it, that we see here possibly one of the worst cases of depravity of womanhood, and Jesus comes to her rescue and blesses her and heals her. He commends her for her great faith and for her ability to press through the crowd and believe Him for healing.

It doesn't matter what our sickness is, or the type of sickness, the embarrassment, or the shame that comes with certain types of diseases that we didn't wish upon ourselves. We can come to Jesus and be healed from it. And every woman on the face of the earth can come to the Lord Jesus Christ. Through this woman's healing He has laid down a precedent that anybody who comes to Him with embarrassing menstruation problems, He can heal them. Not just headaches or toe aches, not just other types of easy-to-be-healed sicknesses, but He came to heal us of all of our diseases. Psalm 103:3 says that He came to heal us of all of our diseases. The psalmist did not enumerate only easy diseases, or men's diseases, but he said it was *all* diseases.

This woman came with a disease, hemorrhaging constantly. She was weak, and who knows what the side effects were? This debilitating disease wracked her body mentally, emotionally, as well as physically. She was probably a wreck, but not so much a wreck that she didn't recognize the healing power of the Lord Jesus. And with no embarrassment, she came and touched the hem of His garment. And He, knowing that virtue left His body, turned and comforted her and said her great faith had healed her.

And didn't Timothy, in later years, say something like this: Through faith women would be healed in childbearing, or any of the other ensuing problems that are associated with womanhood, if they believed? Because of the birth of the divine Child, women can be healed of the problems associated with womanly life. Healing is for women from menstrual disturbances and from hemorrhaging. They can be healed.

The Lord led my wife and me to go down to Chile to have some meetings. I'd never been to Chile before, and it was quite an experience for us. We were met by a lovely lady missionary. She took us to a flat, gave us lunch, and entertained us. Lovely lady, lovely hostess! The view from her window at about the twelfth story looked out over the ocean and around that part of the city. It was absolutely delightful. And we enjoyed her company.

While she and my wife were talking about something else, I was asking the Lord how I could be a blessing to her. Was there some word He would have me give to her? Or was there some prayer that I could pray over her and bless her? I almost wished I hadn't asked because the word that the Lord gave me was nothing that I wanted. The Lord, I think, has His own sense of humor. We ask and He gives, but we don't always get what we want. We get what He wants us to have. God gave me a word for this woman, whom I didn't know very well to be able to talk to about intimate things. So with my wife standing there and still viewing the wonderful view out of the window, I simply turned to the missionary and said, "I feel I have a word from the Lord for you." She began to get excited and said, "What's that?" I said, "The Lord has told me that you are only a three-week missionary, that the fourth week you are laid aside with menstrual discomfort, and He wants to heal you."

The look on the woman's face was something to behold. And you should have seen the look my wife gave me! I looked at her, and I looked at the woman, and I wished I could have jumped off the balcony, down twelve stories. It would have been easier than what I was facing at that moment.

Finally, the missionary said to me, "You are absolutely correct. For three weeks I can go all over this nation and hold seminars and minister in churches, but I have to watch my calendar very carefully. On a set date I must head home, for I'm out of action for a week as I go through my menstrual time. It is so painful, so debilitating, and so weakening that I cannot go away from here to have ministry. Yes," she says, "I am a three-week missionary. Three weeks ministering and one week home."

I sat her down in a chair, and my wife and I laid hands on her. Knowing what I have just written in this book, I said to her, "In Jesus' Name, I break the thought in your mind that you are under Eve's curse. You are a part of the blessing of God." And I prayed according to what I have written, and I lifted the embarrassment, the shame, and the pain, and I commanded her body to function as the Great Creator designed it to function. I prayed that there would be a time of menstruation, but that it would be a peaceful and normal time without all the ensuing, gripping pains and spasms, nausea, swelling, and everything that goes with it. We prayed and we blessed her. Then we left Chile.

The next time we were down in Chile, we were ministering and having fellowship with her again, and she brought up the subject. She said, "Remember your giving me a word from the Lord that I was a three-week missionary?" I said, "I remember only too well."

And we all had a little laugh about the embarrassment of that situation. Then she said, "You'll be pleased to know that God heard your prayer, and I am now a four-week missionary. All the drama that came with my periods has now disappeared, and I can keep working for the Lord for four weeks of every month." Well, we rejoiced and praised God for that!

I love speaking at ladies' meetings because I love sharing with them the truths that are written in this book. I was in Houston, Texas, and I was speaking about my three-week missionary. I said, "I'm going to pray for women tonight who are three-week missionaries, and we'll pray that God will heal you from all the womanly things." Of course, the women came up for prayer, and God did some remarkable things.

When the meeting was over, a mother came up with her 22-year-old daughter. In the hearing of my wife and me, the mother said, "My daughter is a two-week missionary. She has two weeks that are a wipeout, and she has two weeks that are good. She's a two-week missionary." I thought that was a cute way to put it. It was so descriptive, and yet so sensitive. And so, I prayed that all the enemy's lies that he'd put upon us, the lies that had superceded what Jesus would have for our body would be removed.

The next time I was in Houston, the mother brought the girl back to me and said, "Do you know what God has done? My daughter is now a four-week missionary!"

This is symbolic of what God is doing for people when they appropriate what God has said in His Word—when they believe that God has come to set them free, that their bodies are the temple of the Holy Spirit, that they can take off what satan has put on them, that they can have what God desires them to have, and that they can be all—body, soul, and spirit—that God intended them to be.

God has a design, a pattern, and a plan for your life and for the functions of every part of your body. Because you are female, you are no less a part of the body of Christ. You are a glorious part of the body of Christ. Take your rightful place. Believe your Bible right to be healed and touch the hem of His garment. God can touch you now. Say this prayer with me:

In Jesus' Name, I take off what satan has put on me. I take out of my life the lies of the medical profession, the lies of my mother, and the lies of my grandmother. What other women have told me about the pain, the agony, and the shame of being female, in Jesus' Name, I put it on the Cross, and I lift it off. I am not going to have the pain, the shame, the cramps, the hemorrhaging of yesteryear. I am going to be as the Master Designer has designed my body to be. I am going to be perfect in every way. I thank You, Lord, for this healing and the understanding of health for my body, in Jesus' Name.

CHAPTER FIVE

Menopause

When Jesus Christ went to the Cross, the Bible tells us clearly that He bore our sins, our shame, our sicknesses, and our diseases. Isaiah 53 brings that out; so does Matthew 8:17. And Acts 10:38 says that Jesus went about healing the sick and all who were oppressed of the devil. Jesus came to alleviate, to lift off, to release. He came to give life and hope and health and blessing, to lift off the curse and to remove the power of sin and shame. He came to make us whole—not to pull us down, but to lift us up. First Peter 3:24 says that He bore our sins and sicknesses. That means there was a transference.

I think there's a little key here for us to look at. When we consider our salvation, we should think about a transfer. First Peter 5:7 explains it as "casting all our care upon Him." Somehow there is a casting off us, a releasing of our problems, from our emotions, from our mind, and letting them go. We release them to Him. We transfer them to Him. The Scripture says our sins and our iniquities were laid on Him, transferred to Him.

There is a beautiful type of this in the Old Testament in the book of Leviticus, chapter 16. Verses 21 and 22 show us what salvation is for us and the transference of our problems to God: *Aaron shall lay both his hands on the head of the live goat, and confess over him all the iniquities of the children of Israel, and all their transgressions, in all their sins, putting them upon the head of the goat. . . . And the goat shall bear upon him all their iniquities.*

Now all Aaron did was lay his hands on the head of the goat, and he confessed the sins of the people, putting their sins, iniquities, and transgressions on the head of the goat, and the goat bore them away.

Here is a remarkable spiritual truth for us. As we confess our sins to the Lord Jesus, we are putting our sins upon Him. There is a transference that we must imagine in our minds, that comes from our spirit, our heart, or our mind as we confess our sins to the Lord Jesus. We must imagine—because it's a real thing—that we are transferring our problems, our sins, our sicknesses, and our diseases, and they are being transferred to Him. We're putting on Him the iniquity of us all. That's what God did in Isaiah 53:6, and we continue to do it. When we confess our sins, He is just and righteous to forgive us our sins. The confession of our sins to Him enables Him to assimilate them. He takes them, and they are gone from our hearts, from our lives. There's no longer any evidence that we have sinned because Jesus takes them all away.

And so, about our sicknesses, there's also a transference of our sicknesses to the Lord. He takes them. He bears them, and we get healed in our bodies, are forgiven in our spirits, and we have well-being because the sin and the sickness are gone. The power of God is able to manifest in our lives, and we are redeemed. Jesus doesn't still bear our sins on the Cross, but through His redeeming grace, He is able to dismantle sin's power, take it off us, and cast it into the sea of His forgetfulness.

It's a tremendous thing to understand the transference of our guilt and our shame to Christ. Why should we bear it when He has already borne it? Why should we have it when He wants it? So we give Him our sins. We confess to Him our shortcomings and our failures, and He takes them. His blood cleanses us and releases us from sin's power, and we are free. And whom the Son sets free is free indeed (see John 8:36).

One Easter Sunday evening I was teaching this to my church—the transference—the fact that Jesus came to take our sicknesses, our diseases, our sins, our guilt, and our shame. At the end of the meeting, after I had explained all of this, we had a different type of altar call. I just simply said to the people, "Give Jesus your sins.

Confess them to Him. Under your breath just say, 'Lord, this is my fault. This is my failing.' And give it to Him. Imagine that He's standing there in front of you. Just let Him have it. Confess it and let Him bear it for you."

We had a lady in the church who was going through menopause, and she came to us and she said, "Pastor, I'm just having all sorts of problems. I'm hemorrhaging like crazy. I can't stop it. I've been to the doctor. I've been on tablets. He has done all he knows to do, and I've had eighteen months of this dreadful hemorrhaging."

This lady came to me several times for prayer, and we prayed and prayed. The story in Matthew 9 of the woman with the issue of blood—we prayed it, we quoted it, and nothing happened. I was very disappointed because I was in the experimenting stage at that time, testing these truths. I was praying for women. We were seeing some good results, but this was the first one of this nature that I had come across.

On this Sunday night, when I gave this message on the transference of our problems to Jesus, at the end of the meeting, this lady was there bouncing around. Before, she could not dance before the Lord. She could not become physically involved in worship, raising her hands and clapping and rejoicing as she normally did, because her body was so weak. She was a schoolteacher, on her feet hours each day, and it was just sapping her life and her energy away. But this Sunday night she was happy and skipping. She came up to me and said, "Do you know what has happened to me tonight?" I said, "No, but something has."

She said, "I had a vision of Jesus, and He came and walked in front of me. Then He turned and said, 'Give it to Me.' I said to Him, 'Give You what?' And He said, 'Give Me your sickness.' I said, 'Lord, I'm not sick.' He said, 'Yes, you are. Give it to me.' Then all of a sudden, as He started to move away, I remembered the hemorrhaging. I was in menopause, with all sorts of problems. And I said, 'Jesus, here it is.'"

She said that she caught hold of her blouse and pulled, as it were, her menopausal state, and she gave it to Jesus, and Jesus took it and went. She said immediately the power of God came into her life. Her body was touched with His healing power. She felt a change in her body and was so excited. The heaviness had lifted and she was rejoicing. The next Sunday, there she was, stepping out into the aisle of the church, dancing and rejoicing before the Lord. And I couldn't help but laugh to myself, *Yes, it works. The power of God works. She has transferred her sickness.*

People began to be healed all over the place as we continued to see people transferring. We asked Jesus to take our sin; we cast our cares upon Him. We can cast our sicknesses upon Him because He came to bear them. He came to give us gifts and life and health and blessing.

Give Jesus your doubts. Cast your cares upon Him. Yield to the grace of God that He will impart into your spirit, and transfer to Him the negativity, the doubt, the hemorrhaging, the pain, and let Him bless you. He never, ever intended your reproductive parts to be full of disease. He came to heal you and give you health. There's healing for women in the Cross. Jesus Christ came to make women whole.

CHAPTER SIX

Blessing for your Reproductive Parts

In Genesis 49, we find that Jacob gets all his family together and gives them their blessings. For those who may not be fully aware of the covenants of God, God made an Abrahamic covenant in which He gave Abraham the promise that through him all the nations of the earth would be blessed. That was again established with Isaac, Abraham's son, and it was reaffirmed to Isaac's son, Jacob. Abraham, Isaac, and Jacob are the custodians of the promises of God concerning the coming move of the Spirit into the new millennium that God will produce, possibly in the near future. So this promise of Abraham snowballed to Isaac, snowballed on to Jacob, and it became more distinct and greater with each of the ensuing generations.

We come to this great chapter of Genesis 49, and we find that the blessing of the Lord through the patriarchs—Abraham, Isaac, and Jacob—is perpetuated in Joseph. There is a remarkable Scripture in verse 26, <u>NKJV</u>: *The blessings of your father have excelled the blessings of my ancestors.* Jacob is saying, "What Abraham and Isaac gave to me, Jacob, was absolutely awe-inspiring, but the blessings of your father—Jacob to Joseph—are going to surpass everything that I have received from Abraham and Isaac." The triune blessing of Abraham, Isaac, and Jacob was going to be perpetuated and extended from those three to Joseph. The triune blessing of Abraham, Isaac, and Jacob was now going to be extended and snowballed to Joseph. And that's why Jacob said, "The blessings of your father have excelled the blessings of my ancestors." In other words, he was saying, "Joseph, here comes the greatest blessing to any person or individual that has ever been given up until this time."

And so the compounded blessing of Abraham, Isaac, and Jacob is compounded to Joseph so that he would be the recipient of blessings and power as none of the other three patriarchs had ever been.

Joseph received the blessing. And it was quite staggering. It says at the end of verse 26, NKJV, . . . *up to the utmost bound of the everlasting hills. They shall be on the head of Joseph, and on the crown of the head of him who was separate from his brothers.* The whole of this blessing is one of fruitful boughs by a well whose branches run over the wall, that he would be afflicted by others and shot at and hated, but that the arms of the Lord—the hand of the Lord—would be mighty upon him and that he would have the blessings of the Almighty (see vv. 22-25).

Read with me verse 25, NKJV: *By the God of your father who will help you, and by the Almighty who will bless you with blessings of heaven above, blessings of the deep that lies beneath, blessings of the breasts and of the womb.* Well, isn't that unusual—the greatest compounded blessing that was given to Abraham, Isaac, and Jacob concerning birth, death, resurrection, and the ongoing building of the kingdom of God; included in this great, futuristic blessing was the patriarchal blessing upon the breasts and the womb.

So, everybody who receives part of the covenant of God has blessed breasts and blessed wombs. I'm sure that nobody has heard a message on the blessing of the breasts. We have the blessings of the sleep. And one of my pastor friends was part of a unified gathering of different churches where they blessed the roads, they blessed the planes—they blessed everything! But God singularly brings the spotlight of His attention to the blessing of the breasts and the blessing of the womb. Isn't that unusual, when we consider the magnitude of what God is doing through His creation and redemption!

So, every woman who reads this book should lay her hands on

her breasts and say, "My breasts are blessed." She should lay her hand on her tummy and say, "My tummy is blessed." Gone are all the polyps and the fibroids, because those are not the blessing of God. Gone is the hemorrhaging. That's not the blessing of God. Gone, now, are all the menstrual things that cause problems in your body. Your tummy, your womb is healed by the power of God. It's blessed—you have a blessed womb. You have blessed breasts.

We were preaching in one particular church in Texas, and we were telling people to believe for healing. A couple of meetings went by, and this lady and her husband came up to me, beaming. With her husband and one of the other pastors standing with me, this lady began to tell us her story, how her breasts were knotted and gnarled and caused her pain. She'd gone to the doctor, but they couldn't give her anything. She'd taken tablets to relieve the pain, but the knottedness of her breasts was ugly. To wash them was agony; they couldn't be touched. Just to turn suddenly often brought excruciating pain to her body. She had breasts that were not blessed.

This particular morning, as she'd had her shower and was getting reading to go to work, the word of the Lord came into her heart that I'd spoken on: there are blessings for your body and healing for your body. She looked in the mirror and saw that her breasts were not knotted any longer. She touched them. Where before they had been tender and sore, now they were normal. No more knots, no more lumps and bumps, but perfect healing. Her eyes sparkled as she told me that Sunday morning what God had done—blessed her breasts.

God wants to bless your breasts. The newspapers tell us that about one woman in five is going to get breast cancer. The United States figures are a little lower than those of England. But England and America have issued numbers that support what I have stated, that one woman in five is going to suffer with breast cancer. They are advertising all the time, "Come and have a breast X-ray and have Pap smears." And I'm not against either of those things. But the Church has a better hope than Pap smears and breast X-rays. Have them, by all means, so that you can keep a running check on your body, but you've got a promise that is part of the covenant of God—and just because it's written in the Old Testament doesn't mean to say that it's not of God, because it says in Romans 4:14

that Abraham is the heir of the world.

The promises given to Abraham were New Testament promises. And the promises given to Isaac and Jacob and to Joseph bring out the fact that there's healing for women's breasts and healing for women's wombs.

Eve's curse has been broken. Eve's sin and transgression has been forgiven. The consequences have been taken away and there is healing for you, because we are breeding a new race of women who have their names written in the Lamb's Book of Life and are part of the everlasting covenant that God has made with them. Enjoy your blessed breasts and your blessed wombs.

If the statistics are correct, then Christian women all over the world are in danger and at risk. I believe that the Gospel of Jesus Christ teaches us that there's healing for women in the Cross and they should be free from the traumas and the anxiety of thinking that these diseases will come upon them. None of these diseases should come upon any one of us.

Even if there are heredity problems in your family, you don't belong to your natural family; you belong to the Father—the family of God—and He is your Father in heaven. And you have entered into an agreement and into covenant relationship with Him.

We can program our minds, renew our minds to the promises of God and believe to receive the redemptive power of God and that the blessing of the Lord will come upon our bodies—which are temples of the Holy Spirit. We can come into health and dignity and believe that the power of God will smite every sickness and every disease because Jesus was smitten, He was stricken by God. And we are able to enjoy, now, the liberty and the freedom of having happy breasts and happy wombs.

God made it very clear through the prophet Jacob that the covenant that passed from Abraham down to Joseph—these promises—excelled everything that had been there in the past, and that we can expect a healthy body. The next time you examine your body, believe for change. Believe for health. Expect the anointing of the Holy Spirit as you lay hands on your own body. Every time you shower or bathe, you should believe, with the laying on of your hands, that there's health and healing and blessing.

It may not all happen at one time. It may not happen immediately, but believe for it to happen constantly because our minds have to be renewed. We've been told for so many years that we're sick, that we're going to get sicker, that cancer cells are already in our bodies and it's trauma that will initiate them into action. We've got to believe that there's life in our bodies, that there's healing in our bodies, that our bodies are blessed, and that the anointing is constantly within us.

Your body belongs to God. His Word says in II Corinthians 2:4 that Jesus is the Lord of your body. If He's the Lord of your body, why are other things ruling in your body? You have a right to be healed, and you have a right to health and life.

We find a great story in Luke 13:10-13, <u>NKJV</u>. The story is about the woman who was in the synagogue on the Sabbath day. Verse 11 says, *There was a woman who had a spirit of infirmity eighteen years, and was bent over and could in no way raise herself up.* We sometimes have a problem with sickness. We think it's all biological, that there are human sicknesses that are common to all—a biological thing, a normal, natural thing of nature. That's not what the Bible says. Here is a sickness, a woman bowed over eighteen years, and she had what the Bible says was a spirit of infirmity. So, the spirit of infirmity—a demonic spirit of infirmity—had entered her body and caused her to be bent over, and she could in no way raise herself up.

How many people have a sickness, a disease, a problem—maybe you've had prayer, maybe you've believed God, maybe you've had a great physician, you could even have had an operation—and you're no better because a spirit, a demonic spirit of oppression, has come upon you. It's called a spirit of infirmity.

And she *could in no way lift herself up*. But Jesus came along. When He saw her, He called her over to Him. He didn't despise her because she was female. He didn't say, "I'll have nothing to do with you, lady. Move out of the way." Jesus saw her and He called her over (see v. 12).

In verse 13 He laid His hands on her. What's more, He touched this woman. Jesus was breaking all the rules that the religious bigots had set up. Where does it say that Jesus can't touch this woman? He brought dignity back to womanhood. He brought love back to her. There was acceptance. He broke the power of rejection and said, "Woman, come to me."

Women all over the world are beginning to come to Christ. There are more women in the kingdom of God than men because men are hard of heart. Men are more involved with money and sports and their reputations than with God, and with their sin rather than coming to Christ. Women are more sensitive and, therefore, more sensitive to God. And He calls women to Him.

He's calling you to come to Him today. He wants you. He doesn't care what your sickness or your problem is. You come. The woman taken in adultery, He came and He brought release to her. He wants you. Come to Him. He loves you just as you are. He has the ability, the power to love you. He will not condone your sin. He doesn't want you to be a sinner. He doesn't want you to continue the way you're living, but you come to Him. He's calling for you. Come to Him today. Come now, while you're reading this. Say, "Jesus, I come to You," because He's calling you. Why? Because He wants you. "But I'm a woman." Great! That's why He wants you. He wants you because you are a woman.

Jesus spoke against the leaders of the synagogue, and He called the lady to Him: "Come over to me." And He laid His hands on her, and immediately she was made straight (v. 13). He loosed the woman from the spirit of infirmity. The bondage that satan had put on her, Jesus took off her.

And in Jesus' Name, the bondage that satan has put on you, we take off you. The sickness he's put on you, we take off you. We bind the spirit of infirmity, and you are loosed from your diseases. You are loosed from your sickness.

Verses 14-16 say, *The ruler of the synagogue answered with indignation, because Jesus had healed on the Sabbath; and he said to the crowd, 'There are six days on which men ought to work; therefore come and be healed on them, but not on the Sabbath Day.' The Lord then answered him and said, 'Hypocrite! Does not each one of you on the Sabbath loose his ox or donkey from the stall, and lead it away to water it? So ought not this woman, being a daughter of Abraham, whom satan has bound—think of it—for eighteen years, be loosed from this bond on the Sabbath?'*

What Jesus was saying was pretty strong. It's written in red in our Bibles, the words of Jesus. He said, *Ought not this woman be healed?* She had a right to be healed. Jesus was defending her right to be healed. He rebuked the ruler of the synagogue with Scripture, demanding that she be healed because she was the daughter of the man who had the promises, Abraham. He also could have said Isaac, Jacob, and Joseph. And He could have said, "Ought not this woman be healed in her breasts and her womb?" Not only healed in her back but all the other organs that satan had bound—the spirit of infirmity that bound her. Jesus said she had a right to be free, and you have a right because you're a daughter of Abraham.

In the New Testament, in Galatians 3:29, <u>NKJV</u>, it says, *If you are Christ's, then you are Abraham's seed, and heirs according to the promise.* So, we are Abraham's seed: every man, woman, and child who has received Jesus Christ as their personal Savior. Jesus said to this woman, "Seeing that you are Abraham's seed, you are an heir of the promise." And He said to satan, "You have no right to be here, so I loose you off this woman because she has a right to be healed because of her heritage," and so she inherits the promise of God. Healing became her lot. The woman was immediately released from the demonic pressure. Her body was immediately healed, and she glorified God because Jesus recognized the covenants of Abraham, Isaac, Jacob, and Joseph, and He healed the woman.

What the rulers were really saying was, "This woman has no right to be healed. This is the just judgment of God upon her." But Jesus came in and spoiled their ideology of trying to suppress women and keep them down by saying that all their womanly problems were part of the curse of the Mosaic Covenant.

Never, never, never, never—the Bible never says that woman is cursed, that woman is lesser, that woman is subject to every whim and wish of man. But woman is being made into the glory of God, and Jesus defended her right to be healed. "Ought not this woman be healed?"

To women who are reading this book, if you know Jesus Christ as your personal Savior, "Ought not this woman be healed?" And don't say, "Aw, but you don't know the pain I'm suffering." This woman had pain. This woman was demonically oppressed, and Jesus said, "I've come to loose you, woman, so that you can enjoy the blessing of the Lord,—*it maketh rich, and he addeth no sorrow*" (Proverbs 10:22).

What a promise for women, to come into fullness in the most intimate areas of your life, to enjoy the blessing of the Lord upon all of your body, all of your soul, all of your spirit, and all of your mind. Gone is the torment, the trauma, the marks on the calendar that remind you of how long you've got to go in your cycle. The healing and the blessing of God will bring you back to the divine order, according to the pattern that was manufactured into Eve as she was brought forth out of Adam's rib. The perfection of holiness and the faith of the Lord Jesus and a good body, blessed breasts, blessed wombs, and the glory and the blessing of the Lord can rest upon you. I dare you to believe the promise of God!

So, we have to renew our minds because we've been told for so long how bad life is going to be. And as we get older, I believe that we have to eat right. There are certain foods that, in our modern society, are too fatty. There's too much cholesterol, and we should eat the right foods. Certain foods don't agree with certain body types. And I believe there's healing for all of that. There's healing for your appetite. There's healing for your menopause, for your menstruation. There's healing for every part of your being. Your reproductive system was created by God, and it needs to be respected.

I think we all should learn about nutrients and understand minerals so we can have proper food intakes. And we shouldn't always eat at the take-out places or the fast-food restaurants. Some people don't eat vegetables, some don't want greens. A certain amount of meat is good for us. And those who want to move in the power of the Spirit should have plenty of sleep. Sleep is a healer. There's nothing wrong in enjoying good food, healthy bodies, and having a clear, crisp, sharp mind so that we won't be falling for all of the devil's schemes and old wives' tales that have been handed down from the past.

One man was watching his wife put a leg of meat in the dish—a leg of lamb—to be cooked. He noticed that she cut part of the leg in half, or about one-third down. And he said, "What are you doing that for?" She said, "I don't know. I always saw my mother do it this way, so I guess it's the right way." So, the next time this young man saw his mother-in-law, he said to the mother-in-law, "Why do you cut the leg like that when you put it in the dish?" And she said, "I don't know. I always saw my mother do it like this."

And so when he had an opportunity to talk with grandmother, he said, "Why do you do that? Is there some special reason for cutting the leg off at that point and putting it in the pan?" And she said, "Yes, of course there's a reason. I did it like that to fit it into the dish." So, here we find the daughter and the granddaughter doing things that they thought were going to help the leg of lamb to cook. They didn't know that it had originally been done to fit it into the dish!

How many times have we trimmed our thoughts to fit the experience of somebody else's imagination? The Word of God is clear. The truth will make us free (see John 8:32). There's healing for women in the Cross. The blood of Jesus Christ is a full atonement to purchase us and redeem us so that satan's hand has to be taken off of us, and he can take his sickness and his disease with him when he goes!

And that brings us to the breasts, to the womb, to the reproduction organs. Our whole life is in Christ.

How to Deal With Your Problems— The Technique of Deliverance From Sorrow

We're living life today taking too much for granted and easy "believism." You push a button and you can get instant coffee. There's instant everything: instant pudding; instant tea; take your meal out of the refrigerator, put it in the microwave, and eat. We don't want to go through the stages of preparation. Therefore our spiritual experience, our healing, and our walk with God is, "if we don't get it when we press a button, then we don't want it." We want our pastor to carry the revelation in his bag and give it to us like cattle that are fed from a trough. We don't want to forage for it. So the methods we use in coming into an area of wholeness don't work, and we become discouraged and doubt the Word of God.

But there are ways and skills we need to develop in coming into the presence of God. Sin is an offense to God, and sickness very often is a consequence of that sin. Jesus said to the man in John 5:14, <u>NKJV</u>, *Go your way and sin no more lest a worse thing come upon you.*

Not always, but very often, sickness is a consequence, somewhere, of sin. It could be hereditary—something that one's forbearers have done—and the consequences of that sin have never been atoned for. Nobody has ever repented for it, and therefore, the consequences of that sin come down the family line, whatever the problem may be. It could be stealing; it could be divorce; or some other debilitating sickness or disease. And it's there as a spirit of infirmity that passes on from one generation to the next until some-body comes before God and says, "I repent of that sin."

We may not know the sin because of the years that have passed, but we can make atonement for it by coming before the Lord and confessing it to God. As we confess it and say, "There's been sin in my family line—it could be my father, my grandfather, or others that have brought your disapproval. I seek the pardon from that sin, and release from the power of that sin, and from the hereditary nature of that sin and that sickness. And I claim the healing power of Jesus and the forgiveness of the Lord Jesus Christ in this matter." Of course, there's much argument about this concept, but the Scriptures are there.

Over the years, even successful ministries have found that they have a ball and chain around their leg and haven't been able to figure out how to get released from it. They failed to recognize that it comes from somewhere in the past.

You go to the doctor, and the first thing he'll say to you is, "Does your father or mother have this same problem? Your grand-father? Is there any history of this disease in your family line?" Even the medical profession recognizes the transference of sickness and diseases from one generation to the other.

And here we are, as the church of Jesus Christ. We refuse to acknowledge that some of these things are our lot, also. If we can get blessings from Abraham, Isaac, and Jacob, then the sicknesses and diseases that have been brought upon a particular generation can drift on down through other generations. If you don't believe it, just have a look at history. Have a look at your family and see the problems that come down.

Even birth defects. I have, behind my right knee, a vein that sticks out a little bit more than the others. And when I have shorts on, it's evident. My oldest daughter—when she walks and she's in shorts, you can see her vein sticking out exactly the same as mine. My younger daughter—I have a finger that when I point it, it points crooked. So we often laugh together, and I say that this is a hereditary problem because she has a finger that's crooked just like mine. I joke that I think I got it from her!

How do we deal with these things? How do we claim and receive our healing? There's a wonderful little verse for us written in II Corinthians 7:10, *For godly sorrow worketh repentance to salvation not to be repented of: but the sorrow of the world worketh death. For behold this selfsame thing, that ye sorrowed after a godly sort, what carefulness it wrought in you, yea, what clearing of yourselves.*

We look at our sin, our sickness, and our problems and we say there's no answer for them. But I believe that one of the techniques that God has laid for us in the New Testament is written for us there; *godly sorrow that worketh repentance.* We hear people say, "If you repent." A lot of people say, "Lord, I repent of that." But repentance means a change of mind, it means to turn your back on it, to walk away from it.

The reason that sin pops up again, recurring to the point of almost torment, is that we come to a point and say, "Well, there's no forgiveness for this thing," or "We'll never be relieved of its pain or its curse because I've prayed about it. I have repented." But the point is not repentance. The issue is *godly sorrow.* We are not sorry for our sin. We ask God to forgive us because we want the benefits and the blessing of salvation, but we're not really sorrowing because we have sinned. We are disappointed because sometimes we are found out.

People will very often say, "Yes, I'm sorry. I'm sorry. Forgive me." They want forgiveness because they want to be reinstated, but they're not truly sorry for their sins, they're only sorry for being caught, or they're sorry because of the consequences.

We need to come back to the beginning and recognize that when we have sinned, we have sinned against God. We have offended Him. Sin is an offense whether it's from you, your family, or some hereditary situation. Sin is an offense. Sin is a violation of His law. Sin is rude in the heart and mind of God. He hates sin. It killed His Son on the Cross.

We must come to God with godly sorrow with maybe even tears streaming down our face because we've offended the Almighty. *I have sinned against heaven and in your sight*, the Prodigal Son said (see Luke 15:21). And David, in Psalm 51, was so remorseful of his sin, to think that he had offended Almighty God, his best Friend. "Wash me, cleanse me, purge me," he said. "I don't want any remembrance of sin anymore."

Repent with godly sorrow, sorrow before God, on your face before Him, saying, "I have sinned." The lighter you treat sin, the lighter will be your forgiveness, because "according to your faith, it will be dealt to you" (see Romans 12:3). Matthew 7:2 says, *With the same measure you mete, it shall be measured to you again.* So, if you have sinned, whether it's a secret sin or a private sin, you've sinned against God.

And if you've sinned against someone else, then first of all, you leave your gift on the altar, and you go to that person, or you find them, or you write them, and you say, "Forgive me, I've sinned against you."

We don't have much reconciliation today, nor do we have a lot of people who are willing to face the issue of godly sorrow. We have to have sorrow in our hearts that we have sinned against God. Once we come to a recognition that we have sinned against Him, it makes us careful that we don't want to do it again. And godly sorrow works repentance, it gives us the ability to cancel the power of sin, and it gives us the ability to lift off from us the condemnation and the guilt that sin produces.

Not only does godly sorrow work repentance, godly sorrow works guilt out of our heart, lifts the condemnation and the conviction of that sin off of us, and it works repentance, which means we change our mind. We won't commit that sin anymore. Godly sorrow works carefulness in our heart and we walk away from the sin, never to return. The work of grace is worked in our heart and we are freed from the power and the guilt of that sinful thing, whether it be a hereditary thing or whether it be something that we have committed, therefore releasing God to take away the consequences of sickness, pain, and disease. Godly sorrow works repentance that brings salvation, and salvation is the word that means healing and total deliverance, not only from the power of sin but the consequences of it, and brings relief, and hope, and the power to bring healing.

CHAPTER EIGHT

The Ball and Chain of Shame

I had a very unusual experience during my time in counseling. A young lady, about 24 years of age, was not a member of my church, but she found out we provided counseling and made an appointment to see me. She came and told me that she suffered from depression and couldn't sleep. I talked with her and prayed with her, and she came back the next week and the following week.

After quite a few visits, I realized that she wasn't telling me all of her problem. When she came in one particular day, she was very distressed. Point blank I said to her, "You have a problem that you haven't spoken to me about. We have prayed, and God has done some good things, but the real issue, the root of the problem, hasn't been discussed. It's useless to continue this counseling session unless you are going to be brutally honest and share your heart with me."

Immediately, she jumped up off her chair, and said, "I am so ashamed to tell you what I feel the real problem is. I've thought about it, prayed about it, and I don't know how to address it." I said, "Go on and tell me exactly how you feel." Then, to my surprise, all of a sudden she was on the floor, screwed up into a small ball. She looked at me with tears brimming her eyes and said, "This is how I feel. I feel like a fetus."

I said, "Why would you feel like a fetus? What has brought this sense of guilt and shame upon you?" She was very embarrassed. She said, "Well, I haven't lived a good life. I've slept around quite a bit. When I get this sense of being like a fetus, I feel that all of the guys that I've slept with are standing over me and mocking me. And I don't know what to do to break the hold that they have on my heart and on my life. They are controlling me, even though I haven't seen them, and I have broken off all relationships with them. I am not in any active sexual relationship now, and yet, I'm hounded by the sins of the past."

As she stayed there, tears coursed down her cheeks. And to be quite honest with you, I didn't know what to do. I'd never met this situation before, so how was I to address this problem of all of these joinings, this immorality, because that's exactly what it was.

Then all of a sudden, the Lord brought to mind Scriptures found in I Corinthians, chapter 6. Verses 9 and 10, <u>NKJV</u>, say, *Do you not know that the unrighteous will not inherit the kingdom of God? Do not be deceived. Neither fornicators, nor idolators, nor adulterers, nor homosexuals, nor sodomites, nor thieves, nor covetous, nor drunkards, nor revilers, nor extortioners will inherit the kingdom of God.*

She was in that situation even though she had tried to come back to the Lord. There was a great verse of hope for her in verse 11, <u>NKJV</u>, *And such were some of you. But you were washed, but you were sanctified, you were justified in the name of the Lord Jesus and by the Spirit of our God.*

That tremendous verse surged into my heart. Then I said, "Do not fear and do not despair, for there is hope for you to have deliverance from this experience."

Then the Lord brought another Scripture to mind because we had to address another situation, *Do you not know that he who is joined to a harlot is one body with her? For "the two," He says, "shall be one flesh?" But he who is joined to the Lord is one spirit with Him.* It continues, *Flee sexual immorality. Every sin that a man does is outside the body, but he who commits sexual immorality sins against his own body. Or do you not know that your body is the temple of the Holy Spirit who is in you, whom you have from God, and you are not your own? For you are bought at a price; therefore, glorify God in your body and in your spirit, which are God's* (vv. 16-20, <u>NKJV</u>).

Here, God is emphasizing the body. In verse 13, <u>NKJV</u>, He says, *Now the body is not for sexual immorality but for the Lord, and the Lord for the body.* And so He is Lord of the body. But going back to verse 16, He says that *he who is joined to a harlot is one body with her.*

I said something to this young lady that I had never said before in my life. I said, "There were joinings in which you joined yourself with these other men, and you became one body with them." There were about six other men who'd had sexual relationships with her, so she was joined to six other men. Her spirit and their spirits were linked. She was one with six others. And goodness only knows how many other women these men had been with. And if that was the case, then their spirits had been joined to numerous other women. The complexity of all these joinings brought about guilt and confusion to this young lady that she wasn't able to do anything about. Is it any wonder that she was confused, suffered depression, stayed awake at night, lost her confidence, and wasn't able to maintain proper eating habits or other normal living standards?

This is the plight of the world today—the immorality, the shacking-up together, the one-night stands, and the prostitution that goes on 'round the world. Is it any wonder that there's a heap of sickness, a heap of problems, a heap of mental disorders, and pill-popping by those trying to get some stability in their lives? It's impossible to do because there's a spiritual law being violated, and it is, *Thou shalt not commit adultery. Thou shalt not commit fornication* (see Exodus 20:14). God kept the sexual joining for marriage so that when a husband and wife are joined in holy matrimony and they consummate their marriage, they become one. The word one is the same word that is used for the Godhead when Scripture says, *The Lord thy God is One God*—made up of a Godhead of the Father, the Son, and the Holy Spirit. They are one in thought, one in unity, one in purpose; they are one. A husband and wife are two individuals, but they become one by consent, by agreement, and by a vow when they are joined together in marriage. They become one, the same as the Godhead.

When a person commits immorality, they are violating the divine unification of life. This young lady had done that multiple times. Is it any wonder that there was no hope, no peace, no joy in her life? She was very ill-at-ease. I had never understood all of these things before. The Lord revealed all of this to me almost in a flash of time.

I left my desk, went around to where she was on the floor, and I spoke and stood over her, because the Bible says to pray over people (see James 5:14). And I told her that the only way out of this situation was to not only confess her sin of fornication, but to renounce the joinings and to ask God to forgive her—not just for the sin, but for the violation of a divine principle of sexual joining.

As she prayed, she named each of the six men. She prayed, "Let that man's spirit be broken off me—let this other man's spirit be broken off me. I break the joinings. I renounce the joinings of these other men to my life, in Jesus' Name." I told her that now there would be an activity of the power of the Holy Spirit and the power of the Lord Jesus, not only to eradicate the immorality out of her spirit and her mind, but a cleansing of her from the joinings of all of these others. There would also be a reinstatement of her walk with God and the building into her life of the righteousness of God.

I don't know whether physically we can restore her virginity, but in the Spirit, I believe we come back to just as we were before the sin. God sees us as someone who is pure. Oh, we know we're not, but because of God's immense ability to forget, He doesn't see us as we were, He sees us as we are.

The cleansing power of the blood is so tremendous. The work of the Lord Jesus on the Cross and the reinstating power of the Holy Spirit is so unique that any devastated, broken life can be united, put together, made whole, and in His sight be acceptable and righteous—the past forgiven, the past forgotten, letting us stand complete in the will of God.

That young lady jumped up off the floor. She blew her nose, wiped her eyes, looked at me with eyes shining, and away she went.

I went back to my desk, and I read the verses—these and others that I've written here. I thanked God that He had shown me a way to make people whole, to bring them to a place of acceptance in their own eyes, to break off the broken principles, and to build righteousness into their lives.

Several years went by, and then I noticed that this young lady had put her name down for counseling again. I wondered what sort of a person I was going to meet this time. Did my technique work? I'd never done it before. Never heard of it before. Never read it in any book. Never heard anybody preach about it. I was walking on water in this experimentation of the work of the Holy Spirit.

She came in and sat down, and I hardly recognized her. Her eyes were beaming like headlights, and her face was glowing with health and confidence. When she came to where I was sitting at my desk and shook my hand, she said, "I've never been the same since that day I came here for prayer. The burden of guilt is gone. The shame has lifted off. I sleep well and eat well. I have better health than I've ever had in my life. And I want to thank you for what you've done for me."

It was just such a delight that she was laughing and giggling. I wanted to cry because I was so grateful to God for the salvaging of this lost soul, and the building of her into a worthy human being going on with God, singing in the choir, and living a fruitful life, abounding in the goodness of God. She then smiled, shook my hand again, took her leave, and she went out into the blessing of the Lord.

There are many divorced people who have a piece of paper which states that their marriage is annulled—a piece of paper that is a good legal document, but what about the spiritual joining? Many remarried situations don't always work. Some remarried people end up divorcing again, and it's because their spirits are still joined to their first spouse. They need to pray a prayer of separation, asking the Lord to deliver them from the joining and breaking of the vows they had made so their spirit can be set free.

God holds us to our vows. Ecclesiastes 5:45 says, *Do not vow a vow. It's better not to vow than to vow and not be able to keep it.* We make vows in marriage, and just because the government gives us a piece of paper when we get a divorce doesn't mean that the vow in the sight of God is annulled. We need to come before God and say, "Father, break that vow. We cancel it with the blood of Jesus Christ."

Then consider the joinings we've had in the past. People who lived in sin before they came to Christ should go through the same process, saying, "Father, in Jesus' Name I break the vow. I break the joining."

I was raped as a little boy, ten years of age. The rapist was my neighbor who lived across the road. He would have been twenty-five or thirty, and to a 10-year-old, that was an old man. We were friends.

One day he lured me across the road to his house and down to a back shed. There he sexually molested me. On another occasion I was lured by an older man, in the nighttime, up a back lane. It was dark and a horrible place, and there he sodomized me.

It has been over 50 years since both of those incidents took place, but not many years ago the Lord showed me that the attacks were still affecting me. I am in no way homosexual. I despise it because God despises it. I don't want it, or any part of another man's anatomy. My wife and I are very happily married. We have a good relationship with God, and we enjoy everything that He has to offer.

And yet I was in prayer that day, and the Lord spoke to me very clearly; as a matter of fact, it was so clear that I saw it in a vision. A man was taking me across the road. I can still see the crooked fence and the old shed that he took me into. I relived that experience as tears streamed down my face. And when I finished, I cried out to God and said, "What are You doing to me? Why are You bringing that back? I never consented to that! He forced me! He forced himself upon me! I don't understand it! What are You doing, Lord?"

He simply said, "Son, those experiences have never been dealt with, and they are affecting you to this day." Before I could say another thing, I had another vision of the second incident. By the time it was finished, I was quite a mess. I didn't understand why, after all these years, this would come back. So I repented for the men; repented on their behalf that God would forgive them for what they had done, the lust in their hearts, and how they had released their lusts over my body. I want my body to be a temple of the Holy Spirit. I want my body to be pure and clean. And now, all these years later—decades later—I was being confronted in the Spirit with these two situations that, in reality, I'd forgotten all about.

Then the Lord spoke to me, and said, "These things have brought shame into your experience, and this is the root cause for the inferiority with which you suffer." I had battled with inferiority and insecurity for years. I had repented of it. I had prayer for it. I had read the Word. I had lain on the floor. I had fasted and done all the biblical things that are supposed to bring healing, but I didn't know that the root cause of my shame, my inferiority, and my insecurity came from the attacks I had suffered as a young lad.

I again spent time forgiving the men, asking the Lord to forgive them and to bless them. Then I asked the Lord to take away the shame. I renounced it in the Name of Jesus—renounced the impartation and the joining of those two men's spirits into mine. I broke the hold that they had upon me and released it to God. I can assure you that within a very short time I felt squeaky-clean. I felt I was born again. I felt so free. Confidence flooded into my heart that I'd never had before.

Here I was, an international minister helping and ministering to others in seminars and conventions, and I was carrying this ball and chain of shame around my leg. I could never work out why, after all my waiting upon the Lord, that I still had this ball and chain. But the Lord showed me that it went back to when I was molested as a young boy. Now I feel squeaky-clean. I feel so beautiful and accepted in God. My mind is freer; my heart is freer—free from the blood of all men. And the impartation that I had carried from those men is gone, and I am free. It is such a delightful thing.

If you've had situations like mine—maybe you've been raped or molested—then you need to do the same. If you've had somebody force themselves upon you, injure you, and bring fear into your heart—at the moment of fear the unclean spirit of that molester enters into your mind and into your heart, which means his lust also comes into your heart.

Have you wondered why you've continued to feel unclean? You've showered so many times. You've put on more perfume. You've had your hair done again. You've gone to your pastor or a friend. You've wept. You've gone through the trauma of it, and you don't feel much better. You feel used, abused, broken, and broken-hearted. You feel destroyed. You feel as though you'll never be able to really face life again because the shame has brought upon you a disagreeable attitude and a feeling of rejection.

You have to forgive that person, as hard as that may be. Forgive them and then pray as I suggest: "In the Name of Jesus, I break the joining of that man, the violence that was imparted to me, the hurt, the beating, in Jesus' Name; the threatening, in Jesus' Name; that the Name of Jesus and the power of Jesus will take out of my life what the devil has put in there. Break the joining, in the Name of Jesus. Take his filthy, unclean spirit off of me, in the Name of Jesus, and break the power of it. Release it out of my mind."

Keep on praying to the Lord, declaring the power of the blood of Jesus over your mind, your heart, and your body. Ask for a cleansing release in the Name of the Lord Jesus. Keep on doing this until you feel it all go, because you, no doubt, have harbored hurt and possibly hatred towards the molester, which is understandable.

There's no condemnation from me about those feelings because they are a natural reaction to the violation that has taken place against you. But once you start to forgive, you allow the grace of the Lord Jesus Christ to bring about a healthy worthiness into your life so that you know you stand perfect and complete in all the will of God. This can be a process. It won't happen immediately. Those feelings can come again whenever you feel things rising in your heart. If they come again, break them off. It's a process of cleansing and restoration.

And the hurt—the wounds of your heart. Jesus came to heal the wounded in heart (See Isaiah 61:1). He loves you too much to leave you as you are! Apply the principles of the shed blood of Jesus, the Name of Jesus, and the graciousness of the Holy Spirit's activity, and you can come to a place of cleanliness and acceptance that is beyond description.

There's a great verse in II Corinthians that speaks to us of the glory of God and how that glory is for our body, to fill our hearts and our minds. We are made to contain God's glory. Verse 18 says that we are going to be changed, or transformed, into the very image of the Lord Jesus from glory to glory even as by the Spirit of the Lord. That's the Holy Spirit's activity ministering to us all the time. Chapter 4, <u>NKJV</u>, opens, saying, *Therefore, since we have this ministry, as we have received mercy, we do not lose heart.*

Be encouraged. There's hope for us. Verse 2, <u>NKJV,</u> says, *But we have renounced the hidden things of shame.* The word *renounced* means "to cut off, disassociate ourselves from." We verbalize our faith. We verbalize, as it were, the power of the Spirit that can cut off the joinings, that can cut off the associations, that can cut off the influence of past things. And even though our bodies are destined to be filled with the glory of God—our bodies are temples of the Holy Spirit—some of the things hidden in the depth of our spirits, or suppressed down deep in our souls must be attributed to the work of shame. Shame doesn't always make us remember the incident that has taken place. All we know is that we feel guilt, which seems to seep through into our subconscious, and there's a sense of unworthiness.

Given certain circumstances, you react. Why do you react? Why do you withdraw? Why is there insecurity? Because there's someone in a circumstance that you're involved in that is similar to the person who brought the initial disappointment to your heart. And because the years have gone by and you have drowned out the pain and the incident is virtually forgotten, the influence of it isn't. The shame of it—to think that you were violated or deeply disappointed or abused or used brings shame: shame that will control you, shame that helps you to forget.

You long to forget, and yet, it makes you reactionary. You don't know why you snap, why you are reactionary or, in certain circumstances or from types of people, you withdraw. It is because of the hurt of the years covered with shame, and that shame has to be released out of your heart. As the Bible says, *We have renounced the hidden things of shame* (v. 2).

As you kneel before the Lord, ask the Holy Spirit, "What was it?" Let your heart be softened. Just let your mind go back. What were the things that caused the shame? And you might do what I did. You might cry your eyes out. You might react to it. But it can be worth it! The cleansing and the release that came to me was absolutely beautiful.

Shame can influence you. It can bring sickness. If you don't deal with it, it can bring sickness and cause ugly things to happen in your life. You might go to the doctor, and he won't have an answer for your problems. But this is the answer. You can have healing and have release. You can renounce shame. You can cut it off. You can deal with it. You can confront it. You can name it for what it is: if it's been molestation, or rape, or some other form of immorality, or stealing, or lying, or cover-up.

It also says, *not walking in craftiness.* There are a lot of deceitful people. We were deceitful. I've been deceitful. You've been deceitful. And maybe we've just laughed at it and said, "Well, everybody's like it. Who cares?" Well, we have to care and we can't be deceitful. We can't get away from it; we have to renounce it. We've got to recognize that it will damn our soul if we're not very careful—and it will bring us lasting sickness.

This is where all your womanly things can go wrong, because of the problems that you generate in your own heart when you let shame stay there like a lump of concrete. You've got to deal with it. Renounce it and all its hidden things. Ask the Holy Spirit to bring out the hidden things: the grief, the sorrow, and the pain. Those things cause pain. Get them out of your spirit. Expose them to the Light and let the Lord Jesus wash them and cleanse them and change you. You have to be changed. Keep at it until you change. You can be transformed by this activity of the Holy Spirit eradicating these things out of your heart.

You can start to feel better. Healing can begin. All your physical activities can begin to be different. Your health can improve. You can think clearer because there's no condemnation. There's no guilt and there's no shame. You've confessed it. You've renounced it. You've washed it in the blood of Jesus Christ, and you're free by the power of God!

Proverbs 12:4, <u>NKJV</u>, speaks of a family, a husband and wife. The verse clearly tells us that the shame of the immorality of his wife will bring rottenness to his bones. Shame can bring rottenness to the bones. The word rottenness means decay, sickness, and disease. Where are most health disorders coming from in our world today? Bones. Right in the middle of our bodies are bones, and our bones are sick. We have sick bones. We don't have fat bones.

I used to laugh when I'd read Proverbs 15:30 where it says that we shall have fat bones. I thought, "Who wants fat bones?" But now I realize that if we don't have fat bones, we have unhealthy, brittle bones that can have osteoporosis or arthritis. A whole lot of other things can set into our bones and cause dire consequences. And so, we want to have fat bones, a joyful heart, a merry heart, a heart free from condemnation and guilt and shame; we want a healthy body. But if there is shame in your life, look out—here comes sickness. You might say, "Oh, but sickness comes from the devil." No, it doesn't. You might say, "Sickness comes from God." No, it doesn't. It's generated by your thinking, by your own beliefs. And it can come because you have not renounced the shame. Rottenness will seep into your bones. And the commentators tell us that this is incurable diseases. Some have even suggested that it's venereal diseases. Well, be that as it may, shame is going to be the thing that you have to deal with to bring about wholeness of soul and mind and body.

A word is mentioned two or three other times in the Scriptures, and each time it has to do with walking outside of the will of God. Proverbs 14:30, NKJV, says that envy can bring rottenness to the bones. A life that's eaten up with jealousy—a person jealous of another's possessions—that person can get sick. There can be a rottenness in the bones of the person who has envy and jealousy. It's a sure recipe for disaster. Repent and renounce envy, jealousy, and pride, because sickness can be the result.

Let's deal with it properly. Let's deal with it carefully. You might need to get with a friend and have him or her pray with you. You can do it on your own in your devotions, but do it properly so that you might come to health. You'll find that your menstruations, your menopause, and all of these other things that hold you begin to change. Your metabolism can change because the health that is in your heart and your mind will be generated through all your body.

In your mind there is a little computer, and as you feed it and program it and talk health and happiness, then your computer can generate health and life throughout your body. But if you think of decay and misery and sin and shame, that goes through your body and that's what happens. It comes from your right believing or errors made in your thinking. God can bless you and help rid you from this.

A young lady who'd had a disappointing life before she came to Christ found that the men in her church made passes at her. She went to the pastor and said, "You know, I thought that when we all became Christians, this sort of thing ceased. And here, in this church, I nearly have to tell these men to leave me alone." The pastor prayed and said, "Lord, how do I deal with this situation?" And the Lord said, "There are still the fingerprints of sin upon her body." We sin with our bodies. And marks, as it were, are left on our bodies.

This young lady was counseled to read Hebrews 10:22, <u>NKJV</u>, *Let us draw nigh with a true heart in full assurance of faith, having our hearts sprinkled from an evil conscience and our bodies washed with pure water.*

We sin with our bodies. We lie with our tongues. We steal with our hands. And we are immoral with our bodies. Our spirits can be free. We need to ask the Lord to purge our consciences and to wash our bodies.

This can be taken as water baptism, and it should happen at water baptism, but sometimes we don't know the truth well enough to walk in the truth. If there are any who feel there's an inappropriate sense or influence about them that attracts the opposite sex, they should ask the Lord in prayer, "Lord Jesus, wash my body in pure water, the water of Your Word, and the water of Your Spirit."

In Ezekiel 47:1,2, pure water comes from the sanctuary. Dip under its cleansing, healing flow. Wash off the fingerprints of all the people who have fingered your body, handled your body, mishandled your body—even the beatings that you might have received from some other person: the hitting, the scratching, the fighting, the sticks, the chains, the belts —the marks that you have on your body that are marks of sin. Wash your body. Cleanse your body from others' lustful, devious hands. Break off the violence.

Again, we can experience the cleansing power of the life of Christ that can set our minds, our souls, and our spirits free, making our bodies whole so that we can walk holy before God. We can be free from the contamination of the past, enjoying the fullness of everything that God has for us as human beings, walking in the light and the purity of His Spirit, with hearts filled with confidence in the beauty and the magnificence of our living Lord Jesus Christ.

This salvation works. Sometimes it takes skill to apply the principles of the Word, but the answer's there. Apply the principles. Apply them by faith in the Word. Believe that God wants you whole. Believe that He wants you free from all of that. Believe that there is power in the blood of Jesus Christ, and that in the Cross there is healing for women. There's healing for all of us as we apply the principles of the Word by the power of the Spirit, in Jesus' Name.

CHAPTER NINE

The Power that Dismantles the Grace of God

The grace of God is one of the outstanding subjects in the Word of God. I don't believe it receives the attention it should because the word *grace* doesn't sound powerful, like the word *power*, *dynamic*, or *awesome*. It is a sweet, gentle word, *grace*. God's throne is called grace—the throne of grace—in Hebrews 4:16. That Scripture tells us that we can come to the throne of grace boldly and *obtain mercy and receive grace to help in time of need.*

The grace of God is available and freely given to us by Him, in whatever quantities we need. There's no withholding of His might or His power from us. We can come boldly, very boldly, and proclaim and declare that there is available for us everything that we need in this life to help every problem that we have. The grace of God is greater than all sorts of sin. The grace of God is His condescension, His willful willingness, and His decision to move on our behalf. We are not worthy and yet, He does it for us anyway. That's His grace. His grace makes us worthy.

Then, because God decided to have something to do with the human race, He decided how He would minister to us. He decided He would minister to us with His love, His power, and His forgiveness. And because He loved His Son so much, He decided that those of the human race who came to Him would be made after the pattern of His beautiful Son, the Lord Jesus Christ.

The grace of God is found throughout Scripture. Ephesians 1:6,7 says that there's grace for salvation. In I Peter 5:5, there's grace for marriage. In II Corinthians 8:9 and 9:8, there's grace for finances. In Ephesians 4:7 and 11, the apostle Paul opens up a great subject of the grace of God in ministry, in the five-fold ministry gifts. There are other dimensions of ministering to people. The famous Scriptures from I Corinthians chapters 12 through 14 concern the gifts of the Spirit, which are called *charismata*.

For the issues of life, it is the grace of God that determines the quality of His abundance toward us, the quality of His love. The discernment of His Spirit to bring us to places of complete victory and healing in Him is all wrapped up in His grace.

But there is a power that stops the grace of God from operating, and it's not satanic power. It's really not the willingness of God to stop what He has commenced, but it is the determining factor of our will—when we decide not to avail ourselves of the freely given, abundant grace of God - then we resort to another method of living.

The book of Hebrews explains it for us in chapter 12, verse 15, NKJV. It says, *Looking carefully lest anyone fall short of the grace of God; lest any root of bitterness springing up cause trouble, and by this many become defiled.* Paul is telling us that there is a power called bitterness that will cause us to fall from the grace of God.

It's not so much that the grace of God stops operating, because God has condescended to give us His grace. But it is that we move away from the outpouring and ministry of His grace so that grace cannot operate. Then we are left to our own devices. We may choose to be bitter over a subject, a situation, or a person. Because of injustices that happen, we may decide to be revengeful, to seek vengeance, maybe even to hate the person or the situation that governs us.

So, there's an anger that comes up in our heart. First of all we become angry and speak of the injustices that have been done toward us. And out of those injustices comes bitterness. Bitterness begins to be a poison, and that poison works throughout our system, and everything we do, say, or touch becomes impregnated with the poison of our own spirit.

In verse 15, *Look carefully lest anyone falls short of the grace of*

God; lest any root of bitterness . . ., the word "root" is really the germination, the impregnation by the seed of bitterness, vengeful-ness, defensiveness, whatever it is that we have done that caused the seed of bitterness within us to begin to flourish and burst into life. Before we know it, bitterness can travel quickly through every thought we have, so that we cannot think on nice and beautiful things, but we keep coming back to the disappointment, the dishonor, the disagreeable situation that we face. It could be any major complication that we are looking at. A person who has failed us. Some business deal that went wrong. Mistreatment from a husband, a father, a mother, brothers, uncles, whomever, and it left its mark. Even though it's only a seed, it germinates in our heart and causes us to begin to move away from the grace of God.

There was something that was done to me that I felt was below my dignity. It hurt me very much. It shouldn't have happened. To this day, it shouldn't have happened. It was grossly unfair. I kept saying to my wife, "This shouldn't have happened. This is disappointing. It shouldn't have happened." And I said all these things, particularly hammering home the thought that the situation was unfair.

About three weeks went by, and my wife said to me one day, "Frank, you're becoming bitter." I said, out of the bitterness of my heart, "I am not bitter." And she said, "Yes, you are." And she kept on telling me that I was bitter, and I kept on saying I wasn't, and we got nowhere.

But one day as I was praying—and having a hard time, not getting through, not getting the answers that I required and becom-ing quite angry in the bargain, because those are all the fruits of bitterness—the Lord said to me, "You should listen to your wife, you know. She's correct. You are bitter. You need to deal with that bitterness. It's getting very strong."

Well, that stopped me in my tracks. First, the Lord said that I was bitter, then He said that my wife was correct! I had found bitterness a little harder to get rid of—out of my heart —than I thought. If I had allowed bitterness to keep going, it would have caused all sorts of problems to come into my bones, and my body, and sickness eventually would have come because there would have been weakness in the knees, weakness in my body. I would have needed healing, and I don't think I would have gotten the healing because at that time, bitterness was the lord of my life.

Is bitterness the lord of your life? Are you vengeful, hateful, or spiteful to those around you? Because of some situation that you face, does bitterness come up? Bitterness can make you sick. It can stop you from being healed. It can take away the presence of God. The grace of God will not operate, and any operation of the Spirit in your life will be forceful and rough. It won't be the sweet flow of the Spirit. You might go to the doctor and he'll say, "I don't know where this sickness came from." But we know where it came from. It's been growing in your spirit. It is a spiritual power called bitterness.

Hebrews 12:14-17 tells us about Esau; how he became angry with his brother Jacob, wanted to kill him, and cried to his father Isaac with bitter tears going down his face, saying, "Father, bless me. Give me a blessing. Don't you have one blessing?" But Isaac didn't have another blessing for him. And so, when he had an opportunity, Esau got four hundred men and set out to kill Jacob (see Genesis 27:41). Esau's bitter tears never brought him to repentance (See Hebrews 12:17). He never found repentance from that situation because bitterness was his lord.

But Jacob came to Esau with repentance and with gifts and begged forgiveness, and Jacob found it. The two brothers were reunited, but it didn't initiate from Esau. It was initiated from Jacob, who had become a prince of God (See Genesis 33:1-10).

God has to deal with our hearts and not just cut down the tree of bitterness, but the ax has to be laid to the root of the tree. Every semblance of bitterness, vengeful spite, hate, and retaliation is not of God and will not be blessed by the Holy Spirit. In the end, bitterness is going to work against you and cause debilitating things to happen in your body. You may begin to walk wrongly and think wrongly, because the grace of God isn't being allowed to operate. My advice to you is to come to the Fountain that washes whiter than snow, and forgive those people who have harmed you, whether they deserve it or not.

Do you deserve the forgiveness of God? Do you deserve all the good things that God has done for you? It's all because of His grace. Ask God for His grace, saying, "Give me your grace, Lord

Jesus, that I may forgive these people who have harmed me. I'm bitter. Forgive me. I am so sorry. I'm sorry that I've hurt myself. I'm sorry that You're disappointed in me. Pardon my transgressions. Forgive me for my sin and forgive them for theirs. And I ask You to bless them and prosper them in all their ways." And after doing this, you can start to see the power of God begin to operate in your life.

In Galatians 5:1-6, Paul says, "Don't become religious. Don't become legal, for we will fall from grace and Christ will not have any effect upon us. Christ will not profit us while we resort to carnal, natural, ungodly, humanistic ways. We have to have *faith that works through love.*" The grace of God will generate faith in our heart that will cause us to love our brother, our mother, our father, anyone who has hurt us—and forgive them. We don't necessarily have to agree with everything that everybody says, but don't—whatever you do—don't allow bitterness to be in your heart.

The book of Ruth tells us of Ruth's mother-in-law Naomi, who went back to Bethlehem from the land of Moab after she had lost her husband and her two sons. When she returned to Bethlehem, the people welcomed her back. But she said, *Call me not Naomi [pleasant]; call me Mara [bitter]* (Ruth 1:20 Amp). She had become bitter. Sir, lady, bitterness cannot be allowed. It can destroy you if you don't ask for the cleansing power of the blood of Jesus to eradicate it from your life.

Legality hinders the work of grace and allows festering seeds of potential failure to take root and choke out the cultivation of graces and the fruits of the Spirit. It is a deadly thing. It can hinder every operation of the Spirit. It can blind you to your goal, the goal God sets for you. And it can blow your destiny out of the water. You must keep your vision clear and sharp, keep your eyes upon the Lord Jesus, and do everything that is necessary to bring your life into the perfect will of God.

CHAPTER TEN

Restoring Our Dignity

Having been many years in the ministry, one of the things I appreciate so very, very much about the whole Gospel of the Lord Jesus Christ is that He wants to elevate us and lift us up. The Lord Jesus hates sin. He died for it. And He hates what sin does to His creation because when His Father knelt down in the Garden of Eden and brought the dust of the earth together into the greatest masterpiece of technology that the world has ever seen—the human body—He created a beautiful man (See Genesis 2:7). Then He created from Adam a beautiful lady (See Genesis 2:21, 22). They were splendid: the excellence of God. He poured all He had into making a beautiful man and a wonderful woman. They were to be the fountainhead of the human race. Ensuing generations were all to come forth like Adam and Eve, every man, woman, and child.

And God delighted in the cool of the day to come and minister to them and love them. They delighted to listen for His coming, they would run to meet Him. They would sit by a brook in the shade of a tree and listen to the birds or watch the animals as they walked and roamed around freely. God poured into them His affection. They would talk of wisdom and great things, and possibly, the plans that God had for the future. Adam, Eve, and God were a beautiful trinity: one in life, one in purpose.

God's heart grieved when Adam and Eve sinned, it broke His heart (See Genesis 3:1-6). God watched the human race as it rose and fell during the course of the Old Testament, and He could hardly wait for the time to send His beautiful Son, the Lord Jesus. And even though Jesus would have to go through pain, suffering, and sorrow, and would have to bear our diseases, sicknesses, sins, and transgressions—and God Himself would have to watch Him go into the grave—He knew that Jesus' life, death, and resurrection would be the restoration of the human race.

To every person who comes to the Lord Jesus and asks for forgiveness and salvation, He is there to welcome them with open arms, like the Prodigal's father in Luke 15:11-32. He kept watching for his son to come up the road. He would go across town and head for the place where the road leads out of town, and that's where he would wait. Daily he would go and daily he would return.

One day as he watched, he saw his son coming up the road. And he ran—this was his boy! The father fell upon his son's neck, and loved him and blessed him. And he had with him clothes for him. He put the beautiful robe upon his son, the sandals upon his feet, and the ring upon his finger. And do you know why the father did that? Because he was going to take his backslidden son and cover his pig clothes and his stench, and restore him into sonship. He paraded his son through the town with his arm around his neck, gleeful and joyful. And as the people watched the son, they didn't see his sin, they didn't see his torn, smelly, old clothes, and they didn't notice that he was bedraggled, because of the grace that covered him. His father had honored him and brought him home with dignity. He didn't mock his son but brought him home into a place of celebration.

When you come to Jesus, it doesn't matter how bad you've been. He doesn't look at your life and say, "You adulterer. You fornicator. You thief. You're a failure. All the good things you could have been, you have failed to become." He never sees your disgrace, or your shame, or your dishonor. He doesn't want to look upon it and remember you in that state.

When we come to Him and ask for His forgiveness or His grace, He willingly showers it upon us. He takes us into the flowing fountain and washes us, cleanses us, renews us, and we come out brand-spanking new. We come out redeemed and forgiven.

Jesus loves us. He restores our dignity. What man has taken from us, what satan has robbed from us, the scars, the bruises, the mourning, the grieving, and the pain we've suffered—He lifts it from us and heals us. He's the one who heals our broken heart. He's the one who takes us out of the prison. He's the one who causes us to rejoice because our names are written in His book. Where there is dishonor, He honors us. Where there is disgrace, He gives us His grace. Where we are humiliated and broken, He restores us and calls us kings and priests unto Him, and He puts upon us a robe. The magnificence of His love covers our nakedness. He calls us His son or His daughter, and takes us into His banqueting house, and His banner over us is love (see Song of Solomon 2:4).

God never brings up the fact, "Remember when you were in the pigpen? What happened to the inheritance I gave you? Where are all your friends now?" He never brings it up because it's been washed in His blood. It is forgotten because it is in the sea of His forgetfulness. He only sees us as we are in His Son, in His house, singing and making merry.

The Lord Jesus wants to honor you and bless you and restore you so that His glory and the light of His countenance can be seen upon you. And you will dance and you will rejoice. You'll clap your hands like the trees of the field when the wind blows and their leaves slap together, and you hear the rustle of the wind. That's how He wants you to sing and be lifted up on hope and joy, because forgiveness is so real. He wants to love you, His daughter. He wants to love you, His son. He wants you to be in the image of His only Son—not on trial, not on probation, but welcomed home.

You are welcome into the kingdom of God! You have as much right to be there as Abraham, Isaac, or Jacob. You have as much right to be there as the apostle Paul or Peter, because we are all there by the grace of our Lord Jesus Christ. He showers His love upon us, and His blessings are fresh and new every morning. He answers our prayer. He looks after us and cares for us. He straightens our path, brings down our mountain, and raises the valley, and He causes our days to be better and better all the time. The Sun of Righteousness rises with healing in His wings as He showers His blessing and His goodness upon us (see Malachi 4:2).

Oh that men would give thanks to the Lord for His goodness to us day by day (see Psalm 107:8). God is good to us, and He loves us with all His heart!

CHAPTER ELEVEN

The Power of Choice

A woman was sitting in the doctor's office, being questioned as to what her ailments were. The doctor asked her about different aspects of her health and then said, "Did you wake up grumpy this morning?" She thought for a moment and said—looking him right in the eye—"No, doctor, I let him sleep." Well, I may not be grumpy, but some people have called me dopey. You see, we have a choice of whether we're going to be grumpy, or dopey, or joyful, or sad, or glad.

I guess in a way, every one of us comes from a dysfunctional family; I don't know whether there is any other sort. Father may be overbearing or Mother might be dominating or the children might not get along. Or perhaps there's no discipline. There can be a multitude of things that affect a family. And the environment of our upbringing usually has some part to play in our characteristics.

One of the things that I have found very important to health—particularly in the sensitive parts of our lives, such as our thinking processes and the functional parts of our bodies—is the power of thought. Without a positive outlook, we can't believe for good things and believe that God is going to bless us, according to His Word, and that we are blessed. We can be negative and critical, particularly of ourselves.

Medical science has proven that stress is one of the greatest known causes of sickness. Stress can be brought about by bad news, bad circumstances, a death in the family, an accident, or overwork. A great list could be made of the things that can cause stress.

Some of us put ourselves under so much pressure that we become stressful to ourselves. We wear ourselves out, wear ourselves down, and break down our own immune system so that we become susceptible to colds, or the flu, or sickness. We can build up our own health and strength and well-being by accepting that which is good, upright, holy, and just.

One of the causes for our stress is lack of control in the emotional area. We can be hypersensitive, which will attract—like a magnet—thoughts about what people say that seem to have a hook on them. The look of a person, the seeming rejection that we suffer, can tend to foster and feed a thing in us called self-pity. We can become self-conscious simply because we attract that sort of thing.

The person who has self-pity or rejection is looking for friends. They do their best to attract people, but they actually reject them. They actually push people away because the more someone clamors for a friend, the less they want to be controlled by their emotion. Unfortunately, a person who is hypersensitive—looking inward all the time, seeking approval—is the one who will have bad health, sickness, bad periods, and bad headaches. Often, to overcome this, the person will become angry, sharp, and harsh. They seem to be determined to make their own way in life by pushing others down, hurting them, and pushing them aside in an effort to make it up the social ladder.

I guess we have to nail this down as one of the worst areas of our lives: the emotional stress that we bring upon ourselves. A person can get so sensitive that everything becomes a problem. Every pain is of major concern because that is where their believing is and that is what they produce. Every headache they have is worse than everybody else's. They spend more time weeping in some sort of difficulty or being rejected because of a situation. Sudden trauma and stressful times can cause nausea, trigger asthma, and even cause cancer to start.

We must come to the Cross and believe that we have a destiny that God has mapped out and planned for our future. We must believe in health. We can't allow our emotions to run away with us.

We must not magnify things that people say, and take those things to heart. The fiery darts of the enemy can find a lodging place in people who suffer from self-pity and rejection. Those people may be beautiful people but sometimes, even when they get old, they feel they haven't received the acceptance they require. They feel within themselves that they're never good enough to achieve, to be accepted. It is self-destructive. The anxiety that produces fear brought about by worry and negativity becomes a taskmaster that is hard to move out from under.

A lot of women are in this situation—and a lot of men. But we have the power to choose our attitude, for we can come to the Lord Jesus Christ. There is a redemptive plan outlined for us in Isaiah 61. In this chapter we find there is a spiritual problem, a spiritual answer, a physical answer, and an emotional answer. Redemption is for the spirit, for the body, and for the mind because emotions are centered in the soul. The soul has intellect, wisdom, and emotion. The redemption of the Lord Jesus Christ is for us. It speaks of good tidings to the poor, and of the fact that we don't have to stay poor. We don't have to let poverty rule our lives. There is good news, good tidings, happiness, and rejoicing, because the power of God can change our poverty mentality.

One time I prayed, and then made an altar call at a meeting. A man who was a multimillionaire answered the appeal, which was for those who were suffering from poverty mentality. He was crying. He threw back his head and groaned as the tears poured down his face. I said, "Tim, what is it?" He couldn't have been answering my call for poverty. He said, "I may have a lot of money in the bank, but I have a poverty mentality." I could hardly believe it, but then as I prayed for him and broke it, something happened in his spirit. Today it's not his money that makes him have abundant life, it is the ministry of the Spirit in his heart. There's good news for the poor of spirit, the poor of mind, those with a poverty-stricken mentality of rejection.

Isaiah 61:1, NKJV, says, *He has sent me to heal the broken-hearted.* This has nothing to do with a person's body or with sin. This refers to the traumas of life, the disappointments, the upsets, the rejections, people who have abused us and hurt us, our bodies as well as our minds. Our hearts can be broken, fractured, and chipped by the situations of life. We can be oppressed by the disappointment of failures that we've been involved in. The power of sin can break our hearts.

Jesus came to put our hearts together again. He came to put our emotions in right order in our lives so we can think clearly, not emotionally, but with wisdom and sensibility. He came to loose the captives that are bound by bad habits—bad habits that affect our health—including people who are shut in, mentally, by their circumstances. In other words, those who are mentally tormented. I feel a great deal of mental disorder is the result of wrong thinking. Jesus came to give us a sound mind, to think rationally so that we're not introverted or necessarily extroverted but balanced in our daily life.

The acceptable year of the Lord is a day of new beginnings. This is when God starts to do something that's outstanding for us. And instead of struggling against the tide, it's as if the tide turns and *the blessing of the Lord makes us rich and adds no sorrow to it* (see Proverbs 10:22).

We can't change others, but this is what we try to do. In families, we want to change our husband, or our wife, or our children. We don't have that ability. But *we* can change. We can ask God to proclaim over us that this is going to be a year of acceptance. We can start again. Whatever the past was, don't refer back to it. Believe in the power of God, the day of vengeance of our God (see Isaiah 61:2). He can deal in justice and He can make right the wrongs of our past.

People who deal in injustice will not get away with it forever, because there is a day when they will be accountable to God. They will not prosper if they deal with injustice. What we each sow, we will reap. It might not be this year, but it will happen, and then just watch those people who deal unjustly. Just watch as they come to a sticky end!

Deal in justice. Love people. Hand your problems over to God. Hand the person who causes you problems over to God. It's difficult, but let God deal vengeance where it is needed.

The interesting part of Isaiah 61 is that three times it mentions, *Comfort those who mourn. Appoint for those who mourn beauty for ashes, the oil of joy for mourning.* The definition of *mourning* is "to put on garments for the dead." Maybe you are mourning. Perhaps you've lost someone really close—a husband, a wife, a child, or maybe even a baby that was miscarried—and all these years you've been "wearing" a garment for the dead. You're not living because they're not living. You are mourning.

The Holy Spirit's specific ministry is to comfort those who mourn and to take off the garment—that spirit of heaviness that wraps around your soul so much that you're unable to move freely in life. He comes to take the garment off of you. And to a point, He'll console those who mourn.

He comes to bring a special ministry of His grace to you and take the ugliness of mourning—the blackness, the deadness—from your spirit and give you beauty. Beauty for ashes, because those who mourned in Bible times put ashes on their forehead. Mourners wore black, they wore a special garment for mourning, and threw ashes all over themselves. Ashes speak of worthlessness, morbidity, and sadness.

One of the things that I face most often as I travel and minister to people is seeing their sense of worthlessness. They do not feel able or capable to rise above where they are. They're wearing ashes when they go to bed. They're wearing ashes when they get up. They've got ashes of worthlessness evident all over and yet, the Lord came to lift all that off of us.

We don't have to wear ashes or a garment for mourning in His presence. He came to give us beauty. He came to lift off the self-pity, the self-inflicted worry and stress, the continual mourning from our lives. It's time to stop. It's time to lift it off, because He came to give us beauty, to put sparkle in our eyes, a shine in our hair, a spring in our step, and joy in our heart. It says in Psalm 45:13, *The king's daughter is all glorious within.* God's daughters—and that includes you—are beautiful, glorious, wonderful, marvelous people who enjoy the goodness of God.

The next point in this Scripture from Isaiah is the oil of joy for mourning; instead of the graveclothes, there is to be oil of joy. This speaks of wearing perfume. Imagine the fragrance of the lily of the valley and the rose of sharon; the beauty and the magnificence of the

Lord Jesus anointing your head with oil so that your cup runs over.

The perfumed oil speaks of richness, of well-being, of overcoming abundance. The joy, of course, is rejoicing with mirth and gladness. No more sorrow but approval, the approval of God that we are accepted in the Beloved. Many people flog themselves and say, "I am not worthy. Why would God accept me?" Well, I'll ask you a question: Why *wouldn't* God accept you when His Word is so clear that you are accepted in the Beloved? Jesus received God's approval when God said, *This is My beloved Son, in whom I am well pleased* (Matthew 3:17, <u>NKJV</u>).

Receiving your earthly father's approval is absolutely essential. You may never have had your father's approval. You may have felt while growing up that you were worthless, and that your parents didn't appreciate you. Maybe they didn't appreciate you. Maybe they threw you out of the home. Maybe they didn't want you as a baby. All these truths can be the facts of life. But friend, it doesn't have to stay that way.

I came from a dysfunctional family. My mother did her best to love me and raise me along with my seven brothers and sisters, but there wasn't much love or money or clothes or food to go around. My father beat me all the time.

When I became a Christian, I had to overcome all of those past things in my life. As a matter of fact, one day the Lord appeared to me in a vision and He stood by my side. He said, "You don't love your father." My father had passed away many years before. I said, "Lord, I have forgiven him." And He said, "Yes, but you don't love him." Tears streamed down my face. I had forgiven my father, but I did not want to know him. Then the Lord said, "I want you to love him." And so I began to love my father. God gave me a love for him. I never told him face-to-face that I loved him, but I could have done that because I had my Heavenly Father's approval and He loves me. I am so secure in the love of God. I needed God's love because I had suffered rejection. When I see my dad in heaven, the first thing I do will be to hug and love him.

To overcome my situation, I needed God. I needed, my friend, the Lord Jesus. I needed the comforting of the Holy Spirit to get into the depths of my heart. Not for ministry, not for sharing with others, but just to take the cracks out of my heart and healing the broken-ness, to adjust my thinking away from self-pity. Did you know that self-pity is based in pride? And self-pity attracts depression.

I suffered a lot of depression. Depression leads to oppression and, if you're not careful, it will lead to obsession and can push you right over the edge to the point of taking your own life.

When I began to understand this and realize that the thoughts of my heart toward myself was my main problem, and that it was all based on pride—because pride wants acceptance—I repented of my pride. I asked God to help change my mind—-to change the way that I thought about myself as worthless and useless. I began to see that God had a purpose and a destiny for me. I began to fit into that. I began to be successful in life. I had the same abilities that I had before, only now they weren't squashed and hemmed in and tied down by emotional disturbances. Oh, happy day when Jesus took my self-pity away, when He dealt a deathblow to self, when I died to it, when I stopped thinking negatively and began to think of myself as I ought to think!

Isaiah 61 says that the Holy Spirit is the comforter, and that the Holy Spirit wants to make us beautiful. He wants excellence to come from our lives. He wants us to have healed hearts. He wants our emotions to experience wholeness, and that can bring well-being to us. And be careful of the clothes that you wear. I know some people that all the time wear black: black blouse, black slacks, black everything, and all very dark clothing.

The Bible tells us in verse 3 that we lift off a spirit of heaviness and we put on a garment of praise. The garment of mourning is gone. These verses are intimating that not only is there oil with joy, but the garment of praise speaks of dressing up, with ornamenta-tion, as though you were going out with your best friend. It's good for you to look good. Keep yourself healthy. Eat the right foods. Drink plenty of water. Get good sleep. Believe the Word. Quote it. Believe it. Sing it. Shout it. Pray it. Clap. Dance. Rejoice. We do this when we become free from emotional hang-ups and distur-bances, and health begins to surge through our bodies.

But the spirit of heaviness is quite a different thing. The Hebrew translation speaks of a garment of mourning as a spirit of heaviness.

Discontent is a spirit of heaviness. And bitterness and anger are all part of a spirit of heaviness. When this comes upon us we fidget, we're restless, we become impatient, and we have unaccountable, uncontrollable impulses. We want to go out. We don't want that. We want to eat something. We can't settle on anything. The spirit of heaviness is not just waking up feeling heavy or being lethargic. It can be that, but it is also animation, being restless, disturbed, impatient, angry, sharp, and catty.

We need the spirit of praise. When the spirit of praise begins to come upon us, we should actually stop what we're doing, relax, praise the Lord, and lift off the spirit of heaviness, discontent, and contention—lift it off because it comes from the pit of hell. We don't want that. We are made to be clothed with righteousness, anointed with the oil of joy, and to wear the garment of praise. Then there can be a contentment and a peace that passes all understanding.

Put it off. Take it off. Rebuke it. Renounce it. Declare the peace and the presence of God. Unless you do, the spirit of heaviness is the recipe for trouble and then, when your time of the month comes, you'll find anguish of heart, pains, cramps, and everything else that accompanies your cycle when, in reality, God wants you to be a four-week missionary, loving and rejoicing. All of those hiccups of life you can sail through because Jesus Christ is your health. Jesus Christ is your righteousness. You can put on the garment of praise and you can have the anointing of joy. The life of the Spirit will become manifest more fully as you glorify God and you are victorious over your stress and anxiety levels.

How can faith work and operate? How can you believe for God's best when in your mind you're hatching spirits of agitation and contention? You must learn to focus on the blessing and the power of God, and that's a choice. The power of choice is in your own heart. Determine that you'll live in victory. Remember the Prodigal Son—the father never went down to the pigsty to get him. The Prodigal Son had to determine in his own mind, *I don't have to live like this*. And he got up and went home.

You can come to that same focus, that same determination and purpose in your life. You can determine how you're going to live, and that you are going to be healthy and live in victory. You're not going to be associated with mourning, you're not going to allow self-pity to dominate your life. You can rejoice in the goodness of God!

We had a guest speaker, a prophet, come into our home when we were starting a church. We were doing pretty good. God was blessing us. But I couldn't do anything but find fault. I was finding fault with God, with the Holy Spirit. I couldn't get answers out of the Word, and yet people were coming to our church, being saved, healed, and filled with the Holy Spirit.

Then this man of God came and visited with us. He began to pray with me and said, "I don't know what your problem is, but you have a problem, Frank." I said, "Yes, I know that." So he went away and never gave me any help. When he came back, his lovely words to me were, "I know three people who have this obsession that you have: One's dead, one's dying of cancer, and there's you." Then he said, "I don't know what your problem is, but I think it's self-pity."

Now my church that I was finding fault with had just doubled in size that year. The next year, it doubled again. God was blessing us. And yet, here I was in the pit of despondency. Depression was my brother and my shadow. But when my friend said it could be due to self-pity, I began to examine it.

And I realized that the dominating factor in my life was self-pity. Instead of walking in the victory that we were enjoying and what God was doing in the lives of a lot of people —the miracles that were taking place, the opportunities that had opened—and yet, I was struggling with all this mess in my life.

But I learned that I could overcome it. By the power of the blood and by faith in Jesus' Name, by reading the Word and renouncing—cutting off from my heart and my intelligence—the things that were fleshly and carnal, I began to move more in the power of the Spirit. I began to understand the things of God and began to enjoy the things that God gave us. It certainly was a new day. And it hasn't stopped there. Time and again, I have a confrontation with the Almighty, and I must pray and believe and listen to what He has to say. When I do this, I feel and see greater things happening, and the last several years have been awesome with the manifestation of His presence.

This is why I want you to believe that it is possible for you to come into this manifestation of the beauty of the Lord, the anointing of the oil of joy, and that you can have health in your bones to the very roots of your hair. You can be the blessing and the blessed of the Lord. You are the blessed of the Lord!

In verse 7 of Isaiah 61, God says, *Instead of your shame you shall have double honor.* This is the purpose of God. This is not just a book on the power of positive thinking. This is the Word of God where, when we have tasted the unholy, ungodly dealings of life, God brings restoration and makes it available for us.

Where we have had shame, to whatever depth we've had to go to in our humiliation and the embarrassments and the pains of life, God has come to lift us out of all of that and bring us into a place of double honor. Dignity restored, honor restored, so that we are filled with His life. We rejoice daily in His accomplishments in our hearts. Things start and we are given a deposit, as it were, and God then comes time after time and embellishes the revelation that He has given us. And the healing that we have, it grows and grows within us. We become more beautiful, more holy, more anointed. Then we become more useful, and people look at us and know that God has been at work in our lives. Double honor is your portion.

CHAPTER TWELVE

The Boomerang:
It's Boomerang Time

In the last chapter, I spoke about putting on a garment. It can be a garment of mourning, or a garment can be like an attitude. We might use a phrase and say, "wear it." We wear attitudes. We put them on. We come under their influence and their power. We could also be talking about wearing a mantle, which is really an influence, a spiritual influence. It can be for good or bad, blessing or cursing. Some people have enjoyed the blessing of Abraham. It came down upon Abraham, Isaac, Jacob, Joseph, and even into churches today where they're experiencing the blessing of God—the blessing of Abraham. It is a hereditary thing, *the promise of God [that] maketh rich* (see Proverbs 10:22).

Conversely, there are also other types of mantles. In the last chapter we found that one type could be a spirit of heaviness. Psalm 109:17-19, <u>NKJV,</u> says, *As he loved cursing, so let it come to him; as he did not delight in blessing, so let it be far from him. As he clothed himself with cursing as with his garment, so let it enter his body like water, and like oil into his bones. Let it be to him like the garment which covers him, and for a belt with which he girds himself continually.*

This speaks of a man who loves cursing. What we sow out of our mouths will come back. This is from the Word of God. What you speak out will come back. And for a person who curses, it goes out but it, too, will come back upon his own head.

It's like an Aboriginal boomerang that we have in Australia. The principle is that the hunter picks up the boomerang and throws it out. If he misses his prey, then the boomerang will go all the way out in a wide arc and then it will come back toward the hunter. If he is an expert at it, it will come right back to him so he can put out his hand and catch it. If it hits the prey, it falls with the animal to the ground. Then he goes and picks up his boomerang. He can hunt with three or four boomerangs. He can throw them out and they'll twirl out and rise. An expert can hit all sorts of objects in the air. And if he misses, he doesn't have to go and pick up the boomerang; it simply turns around, swings back, and comes to his hand.

Psalm 109:17 speaks of a person who loves cursing, a person who curses, one who puts his venom and his heart behind it. The cursing will go out, but many, many times it will miss the mark and it will come back, just like a boomerang. The Scripture says, *As he loved cursing, . . . he did not delight in blessing, so let it be far from him.* Because the curser doesn't want people to be blessed, then he is not blessed. He doesn't throw out blessing, so blessing can't come back. Because he throws out cursing, blessing is far from him. All this type of person knows is the sad side of life. Things don't go right for him. Things go bad for him because he's not blessed.

This is the principle of sowing and reaping. If you sow blessing, you will reap blessing. If you sow cursing, you will reap cursing. This is the Word of God. What you boomerang out will boomerang back. What you sow into the field, you will reap from the field. The seed that you sow is the same seed that you reap.

The principle is also true in praising God. Praise goes up to God and His praise comes down upon us. As we sow our tithes and offerings, our offerings can return multiplied. As we share our goodness with others so that we bless them, others can bless us. *With the same measure you mete, it shall be measured to you again* (see Matthew 7:2). This principle is found throughout the Word of God in everything that we do, in everything that we say. And if we blaspheme, then judgment will come back. It's boomerang time.

Psalm 109:18 says, *He clothed himself with cursing as with his garment.* As there are degrees of our sinfulness, there are degrees of our blessing. The Word says that as he clothed himself with his own garment, so he clothed himself with cursing (see v. 18). This is as if an influence has come upon him and he's clothed himself with it: he can't say a good word about anybody; he's always finding fault with someone; he's always belittling them, bringing them down, hurting them, shaming them with his manner of speech; and he can hardly do anything about it. It's now not only in his mouth, but it's upon him as an influence.

But it goes further than that. The Bible says not only does cursing come out of his mouth and he wears it as a garment, it also says, *So let it enter his body like water* (v. 18). So, not only is his mouth affected and he walks in the influence of cursing, but it becomes a power in his life. It's in his body. It nourishes him. He feeds on negativity and criticism, and cursing comes from his mouth, from his life, from his lifestyle.

But the Scripture goes even further than that. It says it's *like oil into his bones* (v. 18). His cursing has proceeded to the fourth and the lowest area—it's like an *anointing* in his bones. It's as if he can conjure up deceit and infamy like you wouldn't believe. We look at him and wonder how he can conceive such shocking speech. How can he conceive such hurt and shame and evil, and have no respect or honor for other people's lives or property? I feel many of the people who are in prison and who are habitual criminals fit into this last category. Degradation of human life is up to the power of your choice. As you give yourself over to an attitude, the attitude will come out of your mouth first. Then it can influence you, and you begin to wear it. It will become a dominating factor in your life like water, or it will become like an inspiration, conceiving of evil constantly.

Verse 19 says, *Let it be to him like the garment which covers him, and for a belt with which he girds himself continually.* In gusty, stormy, wet, windy weather you put on an overcoat—an outer garment—and you belt it tightly around your waist so that the wind and the freezing cold can't get in. So it is with a person who curses and blasphemes. He is cocooned in his own sinfulness and deceit. This is deceptive and powerful.

When a person comes to Jesus Christ, a person who has been

bound by this sort of thing, it can take them some time to bring the anointing of anger and cursing out of their spirit, then out of their body, and then out of their mouth. This is why some people have trouble with lying, stealing, cheating, or cursing because they think, *Okay, now my sins are forgiven.* But it's not the issue of one's sins being forgiven. The issue is, what do you have on? What are you wearing? What are your garments? Are you clothed with mantles of salvation, of joy, perfumed with the anointing of the Spirit? We need to recognize that there are several levels of this that have to be dealt with individually, in prayer and in confession of the right Words of the Lord. God has to deal with all the issues of our lives. This is why it is possible for a person to be saved for many years, but then in their latter years there can be some form of failure.

But don't limit this to only cursing. It can also be immorality. We can talk uncleanness and soon we'll begin to wear it. Then it becomes something that's constant; it becomes an obsession. Or we can start off disliking or gossiping about somebody. Then we begin to hate them. We become jealous of them. We may come to the point where we want to do them harm. Any unsavory, sinful area of life that you want to name, you can put in Psalm 109 in the place of the word cursing. For instance, we can become deceptive because we've lied at school or we've lied to our parents. Through time, in the end, we become liars. We walk a lie. We live a lie. We are deceitful.

It takes more than just saying that you are saved. It means giving your heart to a deeper ministry than just becoming a Christian. It's the cleaning up. Just like when we catch a fish, scale it, and clean it, we need to come to the Lord Jesus and ask Him to take off layer upon layer, take them off of us until we're totally renewed.

Again, we can look at the situation from a positive point of view. It says in the Scriptures that we can become addicted to the love of the saints (See I Corinthians 16:15). We can like them. We can love them. We can bless them. Then we want to do everything we can for them. There is a progression. There is a covering and then it is almost as if we had become possessed—we become what we are doing, and loving God and His saints becomes second nature to us because there's a covering.

Sometimes we are cursed. Sometimes our heritage is not a good heritage: Our parents can curse us, our friends can do the same; or a hereditary curse can come upon our family. We need to deal with these things very carefully because this all works against us in our health.

If there is a particular sickness or disease in the family, we need to go to the Lord and break the curse that's over the family. We don't want to wear the curse. We don't want the anointing of it, the creative nature of it where it keeps on reproducing itself. We need to rebuke it in the Name of Jesus and cut off the family curse, including the disappointment or the disapproval of others. It doesn't matter what other people think. Come into a right relationship with God and His Word and enjoy the health and life and blessing of the Almighty God.

Psalm 109:29 says, *Let my accusers be clothed with shame, and let them cover themselves with their own disgrace as with a mantle.* You don't have to curse anybody. You don't have to bring railing accusation against anybody. Instead, you just commit them to the Lord and say, "Father, You do what's right in their life. I bless them. I'm not going to hold anything against them." They can be doing things that are obnoxious, but just let them go. Say to yourself, *They're not my responsibility. I only have to love them, pray for them, bless them, and forgive them.* This can help you so they do not influence your life. God will then be able to minister to them.

When you put your hand on a person and tell God what to do with them, very often nothing happens. But when you love them, bless them, commit them into His hand, then He is at liberty to do whatever He wants to do. Sometimes our judgments of them are totally unjust. We might be too light in our judgment, or we might be too severe. *Shall not the Judge of all the earth do right?* (Genesis 18:25).

You have to rely on and put your trust implicitly in the justice of God, believing that He will do right. He can deal justly, He can judge where it's necessary, and He can release where it's necessary.

Release people from your heart. Don't let them dominate you. Let health and blessing, good thoughts—clean, holy thoughts and creative words of God permeate your life—and watch the difference. Give yourself a little bit of time and begin to watch the continual blessing of

God that makes you rich become an integral part of your daily life. You will be surprised at the blessings that come new every morning, day after day. Believe and expect to receive the blessing of the Lord.

But, of course, if you're not sowing blessing, if you're not throwing it out, if you're not boomeranging the blessing of the Lord to others, how can blessing come back to you? It won't come back. *Cast your bread upon the water, and it shall come back after many days* (see Ecclesiastes 11:1, NKJV). Give it time to go out and do its work. Give it time to come back to you. And expect to see the blessing of the Lord flowing into your heart, flowing into your home, flowing into your family. *Goodness and mercy shall follow you all the days of your life* (Psalm 23:6).

Take off every oppressive mantle. Take off every negative influence. Break off every curse, every agitation, all anxiety, and trust God with all your heart, for He loves you and wants to do you good.

The realm of the spirit has substance. Hebrews 11:1 says, *Faith is the substance of things hoped for, the evidence of things not seen.* Faith is a substance. The anointing is a substance. Sickness is a substance, a thing, but not necessarily a demonic thing. Sickness is a power within our lives, a destructive power, but it is a substance.

Each word that we speak has life in it. Every word that God speaks has life in it. Each word has within itself the power of its own fulfillment.

When Jesus prayed for Peter's mother-in-law, He rebuked the fever (See Luke 4:38, 39). He rebuked the living organism that was taking her life. The fever could have produced pneumonia or maybe double pneumonia, and she could have died. But Jesus rebuked the fever and the fever left. If the fever is not a substance or a thing, how could it leave? According to Luke 5:13, when Jesus healed the leper, *the leprosy left him.*

So sickness, leprosy, and disease are substances, and we need to kill them, to rebuke them in the Name of Jesus. Not just praying, "Dear Jesus, heal this man," but praying, "Lord Jesus, kill that germ. Lord, we rebuke that substance that it will leave the body, that its power will be broken by the power of the blood of Jesus." Just as sickness has power and words have power, so likewise, anointing has power and cursing has power.

This is why we speak blessing, because blessing has a power to break curses, to break sickness, and to bring life and health. We cover ourselves with the anointing of the Word, the anointing of the Spirit, and we believe in it. It can work in our lives because there's life in His Word, there's power in His Word, and there's power in our words. So we come under the covering and the anointing of blessing, the blessing of the Lord making rich. There's power in words, a power of choice. This is why words hurt us, because there's power in them. If we accept words that are said to us, even negative words, they can begin to affect us, poison our spirit, and bring bitterness and resentment.

When someone blesses you or you hear a prophetic word, receive it. Take it into your spirit. It can bring life, health, and well-being, and give you direction because there's substance, powerful substance, in every word. In each word there is the power within itself to bring about its own fulfillment according to its own nature. This is why we bless others in the name of the Lord. We are boomeranging it out. We are sowing seeds of kindness. We're sowing seeds in finance. We're sowing finance into the work of the Lord, into the ministry. We're sowing blessing into our family, goodness into our family that can come boomeranging back, a bigger harvest than what we sent out. This is the abundance of God. We're sowing into the Spirit and we shall of the Spirit reap everlasting life. These are not just nice platitudes. These are the facts of life!

CHAPTER THIRTEEN

Buffet-ing the Body

In Genesis 1:29, <u>NKJV</u>, *God said, See, I have given you every herb that yields seed which is on the face of all the earth, and every tree whose fruit yields seed; to you it shall be for food.*

When it comes to good health, what we eat is going to determine our health levels. Like it or not, we have to get back to basics. I believe many healings are detained or not retained because the person healed goes back to eating and living the way they had been. I believe many sicknesses and diseases could be avoided by eating the life of the fruit, all the vegetables and seeds.

Different seeds have unique abilities to add nourishment or to cleanse our system by removing poisons and irritants from our blood and from our flesh, Our blood, or circulatory system, is so wonderful—it not only feeds the different parts of the body but it also removes the rubbish, the dead cells that have outlived their usefulness. They're carried from the blood into the kidneys and liver and purified, and then the waste is expelled from the body. The blood is purified and it keeps on doing its work again.

We have failed to realize that God said in the beginning that the ideal way to be healthy is to eat the right foods. Verse 29 says, *I have given you every herb.* We should eat herbs that yield seed which is on the face of all the earth. Seeds are good for us. We laugh when we hear of people eating pumpkin seeds and sesame seeds and other types of seeds and grains. But all of a sudden, in the last few years, we have seen an increase in the availability of whole-grain bread, which is the best sort of bread you can have—full of life. Some seeds are even cancer-hindering. Seeds can cleanse our bodies, help rid the badness in our blood, and expel it from our bodies. Seeds and nuts, fruits and vegetables are life to us.

We should be feeding our children a good plate of vegetables—leafy greens, lettuce, peas, beans, celery, and cucumbers. Even onions and avocados have body-building, quality nutrients in them. Natural vegetables have no additives in them and they are full of life.

We come from the dust. (See Genesis 2:7). God made us out of the same dust that trees come from. Nuts and grass and wheat and oats and barley all came from the same material; therefore, they are made for us. They are body-friendly. They can help purify our blood, put suppleness in our skin, and health in our hair.

You don't get healthy hair from a bottle, and you don't get bright, sparkling eyes because you put eye drops in your eyes. You get beautiful hair and eyes because you have inner health and your body is filled with the goodness of God. And God—not the naturopath—gave you herbs, seeds, nuts, fruits, and vegetables. The less processed the vegetables are when you eat them, the better they are for you. You should steam your vegetables so the nutrients don't go down the drain.

I believe that if we forgot about "fast foods" and all of the rich spices and seasonings, we would be healthier. I believe there would be fewer heart attacks, our blood would be better, and life would be more enjoyable. But we've passed on from one generation to the next the use of high-processed foods which have the quality of life taken out of them. We eat "dead" food. Living people should eat *living* food.

Years ago, when my wife and I got married, we talked about the low salary that we lived on. We were pastors of a small church and we had to work out our budget. We sat down and agreed that if we ate properly, there wouldn't be medical expenses. So night after night we ate three or four vegetables. There would be some cabbage, cauliflower, peas or beans, carrots, and, because we lived in Australia, pumpkin. The yellow vegetables are good for detoxifying your blood. You don't have to go through some special program; I believe that if you eat proper foods, the automatic cleansing process of the blood will be there. Proper foods can help your digestion. They can help your breathing—and your thinking. They can stop your brain from being clogged up. We can be better, healthier people by eating proper foods.

Why are people all over the world turning to this type of lifestyle? We laugh at it because we think that it's "New-Agey." Well, it's "old-agey!" It came from the first chapter of the first book of the Bible where God said this is the way to eat. If we reverted back to proper eating, I believe we wouldn't have so much sickness. Proper nutrition affects your heart, your blood, and your menses. It can give you life that is competitive.

Why has God given us so much water? Because we need it to flush our system, the same as we flush our toilets. We need plenty of water to flush our system. Our bodies are made up of about 70 percent water, and we need to replenish that water to purify our blood. Six or eight glasses of water a day is going to keep us healthy and keep our bowels active. If we don't eliminate waste, the body begins to absorb the waste. We need to help clear passages: nasal passages and urinary tracts need to be clean, and bowel actions need to be frequent.

We need to expel what God wants us to expel. We need to retain what God has designed the body to retain. The body is His temple (See I Corinthians 6:19). It is holy ground. God comes and lives in our bodies. He wants our bodies to work for Him. Our bodies are a part of the kingdom of God. He is the Lord of the body. We should be a living example to others. When people look at us, they should be able to see a healthy, Spirit-filled, Holy Ghost-anointed body.

My wife and I determined that if we ate correctly, we could have healthier bodies. And because we were living in near-poverty, that's what we had. We had food that was nourishing. We had exercise, we had sunlight, we had fresh air—all things necessary for a healthy body. And we fed our four children good food. We made them eat their cabbage, their cauliflower, their lettuce, and their greens. We gave them the lot. We did our best to have fruit on the table, even though fruit was sometimes very expensive. But we didn't have many hospital bills. We didn't have many doctor bills. We weren't on any form of medication. We could afford the food because we weren't paying out money on all the other supplements that we might have needed to bring our bodies back to health. And to this day, we might get a cold like everybody else, but generally, our health is good. Our bones are good. Our eyes are good. Our life is good because God saw that it was good (See Genesis 1:11, 12). He saw that the vegetables and the fruits and the nuts and seeds drawn from the ground, from where man was drawn, would cleanse, refine, and maintain a body to become the temple of the Holy Ghost.

Psalm 139 is one of the great psalms in the Word of God. Read all of it at your leisure, but read from verse thirteen. It says, *For You formed my inward parts; You covered me in my mother's womb. I will praise You, for I am fearfully and wonderfully made; marvelous are Your works, and that my soul knows very well. My frame was not hidden from You, when I was made in secret, and skillfully wrought in the lowest parts of the earth. Your eyes saw my substance, being yet unformed. And in Your book they were written, the days fashioned for me, when as yet there was none of them* (vv. 13-16, <u>NKJV</u>).

Fantastic verses, speaking of David when he was in his mother's womb. David said, *You formed my inward parts.* All our inward parts were formed by God. When you were in your mother's womb, the Almighty God looked after you. Whenever any woman on the face of the earth is having a baby, the Spirit of God is in attendance, because that little baby that is about to be born has the potential to be the dwelling place of God. God wants to see that the baby is made well, that all the parts function well together. I believe that the reason some people are born deformed and with parts missing is because of a chemical imbalance, because of sin that's in the world, because of satanic interference into the affairs of men and women. But generally speaking, God is there, helping that little baby become a man or woman of God.

Psalm 139:13 says, *You covered me in my mother's womb.* God covered us. The Hebrew says *wove,* meaning integrated, cohering, brought together, functioning together. He put us together. Made us. Loved us. Every part of us was lovingly put together. *I will praise You, for I am fearfully and wonderfully made* (v. 14).

I like to wonder how, when I look at my hand and just think of twitching my fingers, I can twitch any one of my fingers! I can cause my hand to scratch my leg or my nose, or I can rub my fingers through my hair or work the computer. How does this all happen? What sort of electronic power is within us that makes us so fantastic? What causes all the different parts of the body—the kidneys, the bladder, the spleen, the heart that pumps the blood, all the other parts of the body—to function? They're there. They function. They're alive. They're warm. They pulsate blood. We are fearfully and wonderfully made!

When we begin to think—the pituitary gland is up there to govern the cycles of the body. It is such an important, most vital part of our whole anatomy. And our toes wiggle. Our legs walk. But I think most wonderful beyond all that is our mind. Our mind isn't a substance. Thinking is not a substance. Thinking is an ability. How did God give us the ability to think, to see, to discern colors and shapes and forms, and to feel and understand the cycles of life? We are fearfully, wonderfully made.

A very dear doctor friend of mine once said that a surgeon can cut, and lance, and take things out and put things in, and do all of those things, but a surgeon can't heal. Surgeons can stitch up a wound and get the two parts together, but they can't heal the wound. There's healing in our body. There's a force of life—the creative anointing of God, the creative breath of God upon us and in us, whether sinner or saint—that can cause healing to come to pass. If God didn't want us to be healed, our bodies wouldn't heal.

When you come closer to the Lord and understand His purposes with His Word, you can understand that His Word became flesh. When He spoke the Word, the Word became the Lord Jesus Christ in the womb of Mary. And so when the Word of the Lord comes to you, it creates life in you. It generates power that throbs through every part of you to make your body such that God can live in it, and you can live for God—successful, prosperous, healthy, wise, intelligent, excelling in goodness to glorify the Name of the Lord.

The psalmist says in verse 15, <u>NKJV</u>, *My frame was not hidden from You, when I was made in secret, and skillfully wrought in the lowest parts of the earth.* God saw your frame, your skeleton. Why do you have so many little bones in the back of your hand, all those minute, little bones that work your fingers? He saw your frame. Doctors tell us that as a baby in the womb is being made, it has little stubs everywhere. Those little stubs just keep growing and growing and some of them form wonderful, working fingers. And what about legs? When they get to the knee, automatically those little stubs—all the mechanism that's intricately worked into the knee—just keep growing down the leg, all those muscles and bones down to the ankle.

Oh, how wonderful is the ankle to hold you, to bend and twist, to hold your weight, to run and jump and skip and do all its different functions! And think about your shoulders, down to your elbows. The little stubs just keep working. Consider the intricate mechanism of the elbow: enabling you to turn your arms around, to pick up weights, to reach up, to stretch down. Then to the wrist, and all the bones that are in it. Then there are the blood vessels and arteries. We are fearfully and wonderfully made, down to our very hands!

Verse 16 says, *Your eyes saw my substance, being yet unformed.* He saw you as a fetus, and in His mind He could see the future. He could see the potential of your life and He began to pour into you His will—giving you destiny and purpose. He put character and ability and strength in you. He put within you hunger and desire so that when you grew up you would be able to function, and you would begin to express your own will. You would develop as part of the very hierarchy of God, growing up to be sons of God, sons of the kingdom, a daughter of the Almighty, bearing His nature, made in His image to bring forth His goodness and His work.

Verse 16 goes on to say that all of these things are written in His book. God is a bookkeeper, and he keeps good records. One day, the books will be opened and God will want to know how you used your body. Have you used your body for His glory? Has His image been seen in your deeds and your thoughts? So you must keep your body well. You must keep it healthy. He will do His part to keep you healthy, but you have to do it His way. I believe that if you eat bad foods, bad foods will do bad things to you.

Satan hates woman. He hates woman like anything, and he must have nightmares about what he can do to women! He's made it very difficult for women because it was a woman who gave birth to the Savior of the world, the Lord Jesus Christ. Satan's failed plan is to wreck the reproductive organs of women, causing them to suffer beyond the norm. He has designed emotional traumas that trigger unwanted responses, causing contention or friction.

We really haven't had our eyes open to see satan's destructive schemes. The god of this world has deceived us well. He has robbed us blind of the pure joys of life: the joy of marriage, the joy of bringing up our family, the joy of womanhood and of mother-hood. The different phases and cycles of life were never meant to be boring or painful. First Corinthians 6:13, <u>NKJV</u>, says, *The body is . . . for the Lord, and the Lord for the body.* We are to *glorify God in our body* (v. 20, <u>NKJV</u>).

I entertained a missionary on one occasion in the city of Bendigo, in Victoria, Australia. I was a single, young pastor. This was my second church as a single man. Willie Burton was a famous missionary who had taken the Gospel to Africa, now over a century ago. The missionaries who had gone before him never made it past the beach. They got out of their sailing ships, rowed onto the beach, and were killed before they got out of their boats.

Brother Burton was the missionary who came after them. After he landed, as the natives surrounded him with spears and wanted to take his life, he saw someone who was bowed over with sickness. Before they could stop him, he rushed over to the person and laid hands on him. He rebuked the demonic power over the man's life and brought healing to him, and the man stood upright. And so the natives didn't kill Brother Burton. That was the beginning of his planting over eleven hundred churches, translating their language into writing, and doing all the wonderful things that he did. He received great recognition for his work as a missionary.

He was also an artist. He loved art. He loved painting. He did do that in his spare time. He came to visit me in Bendigo, and the big house I lived in was available because the owners were away for a few weeks. I was there on my own so I brought him into my house. And it was very difficult for a single, young man to afford to feed this world-famous missionary.

I was thinking of things we could do in our spare time. "Let's go down to the art gallery," I suggested, and he wanted to do that. So we went down to the art gallery, a small one in this mining town. We went from one room to the next and looked down this wall and that. I went a little ahead of him because he admired some of the paintings that I didn't see much value in. I really didn't appreciate art all that well.

All of a sudden, I stood in front of a larger-than-life painting of a nude woman. I looked at the woman and saw a well-proportioned body. I looked to see if Brother Burton was looking at me looking at her. He wasn't. So very quickly I made my escape and went to the other side of the room. It was a large room, and there were a lot of people in the place and lots of beautiful paintings.

All of a sudden I heard a voice calling, "Brother Frank." I looked around and there he was, standing in front of the painting of the nude. He said, "Brother Frank, come here."

All the people in the room were watching, watching Brother Frank come here. I came and stood by him. There he was, gazing, eyes wide open, looking at this beautiful painting, this woman in the nude. I didn't know which way to go or which way to look or what to say! Then he turned to me and said, "Isn't that beautiful?" I mumbled something under my breath. And he said, loudly, for everybody to hear, "What did you say, Brother Frank?" I said, "Yes, it's absolutely fantastic."

Everybody in the room laughed! I was so highly embarrassed! He went on adoring the body in the painting and said, out loud for everybody to hear, "God has made a beautiful body. We are fearfully and wonderfully made." He went on and virtually preached a message to this painting with everybody in the room able to hear. By the time he was finished, we each knew that we had a beautiful and a glorious body! And it is. Our bodies are fearfully and wonderfully and beautifully made.

To be quite honest with you, I have never been back to that art gallery or taken anybody there since. Any missionary who comes by, he can watch television or go read his Bible, but I'm not going to take him to the art gallery!

Our bodies are beautiful. The next time you take a shower and you are washing your hair and your body, give thanks for every part that you have. As you wash your body, give thanks for it. Believe healing for your body. As your hands glide over your body, let it be the laying on of hands, and believe for healing for every part of your body, for every function of your mind, your will, your heart, and your emotions. Let the power of God go from your hands into your own body. Believe for healing. God loves us.

After you've dried your body and if you have some oil handy, get a little bit and rub it into the palm or the fingers of your hand, and smear a little bit on your head. Anoint your body with oil— every part of your body—and dedicate your body and commit it to the Lord Jesus Christ. Don't use your body for unclean purposes. You don't want your person to be handled by anyone but a husband or wife. You don't want any person or any thought of uncleanness or impurity to defile that which God has cleansed.

Our bodies are the temples of the Holy Spirit. Our legs are part of that. Our feet and every part of our being are fearfully and wonderfully made, to be used according to the Bible. And if we remember that, we can live long, healthy, prosperous, joyful, and exciting lives.

We need to study the different nutritional values of foods and what they can do for our bodies, so that we can eat with intelligence to affect the natural cycle of our bodies' activities. We're all different. We could share all sorts of things on these pages but it wouldn't suit everybody. So do a little homework and buy some books that speak of the value of nutrients, minerals, vitamins, and different types of food, and let's eat our way to healing. We can help the purpose of God.

I know a man who had some serious stomach ailments, and he was dying. We had a telephone call, asking if we could pray for him. So we prayed for him and he was healed—a remarkable healing. As people learned of his healing, they called and we all praised God together. It was a great healing.

A couple of months went by and we had another friend call to say that the same man was sick and dying of the same ailment. So this time, instead of just going to prayer, I asked some questions, including, "What's the matter?" It seemed that since he was healed, he had been eating all sorts of junk food and stuff that wasn't healthy for the body and drinking stuff that wasn't healthy. He had brought upon himself again a serious condition that nearly took his life.

I said, "Well, I'm not going to pray for him unless he promises to eat properly and change his way of living. He's just wasting our time. He's a Christian, but he'll go into eternity having not fulfilled the vision of God for his life."

Well—not just because of what I said—he changed his way of living and eating. He's alive today because he's eating and living differently.

I think this renewal that has been sweeping the world is ordained of God. The Bible is filled with verses which tell us to rejoice. Many times in his letters Paul said to rejoice. David wrote psalm after psalm about rejoicing, but we don't do it. When we're sad, we don't rejoice (See James 1:2). We let sadness creep on us, overcome us, overwhelm us, and we wonder, *What's wrong with me?*

We need to praise God because He's worthy. He's worthy of our praise. Praise Him. Love Him. Rejoice in Him. Have an intimate relationship with Him. He's beautiful. He's our Father, and His Son is glorious. The Holy Spirit is our comforter. What a magnificent Godhead we have! Paul said in Philippians 4:4, *Rejoice in the Lord always. Again I say rejoice!* We need to clap our hands. It can break stress. It can break the cycle of worry and anxiety. The joy of the Lord is our strength, and the joy of the Lord can also help us break stress cycles (See Nehemiah 8:10).

One doctor prescribed for his patients, "One good belly laugh a day." If we did a little laughing, we might smile a bit more. We might laugh at a joke, but we don't really express the joy of the Lord day by day as we should. In a meeting, we might have a spiritual laugh. But do we truly laugh? Are we happy? Are we generous in our liberty of praise, of worship? *A merry heart doeth good like a medicine*, says Proverbs 17:22. It can bring health to the bones. So instead of getting osteoporosis, we can have healthy bones through laughter. The joy of the Lord and the laughter of that joy can bring God's goodness into our lives.

It's well known that most women between the ages of forty-five and fifty-five begin to produce less estrogen. This triggers the onset of menopause and with that, often a number of distressing symptoms, such as hot flashes, irregular bleeding, and unpredictable mood swings.

Up until recently, menopause was a matter of "grin and bear it; there's not much you can do about it." Of course, now, you can go to the doctor and sometimes get an injection or some tablets to help replace the hormones the body is no longer producing. But there is another type of hormone replacement therapy. Did you know that for thousands of years, people in Asia have eaten a diet rich in soy? As a matter of fact, Asian women forty-five and over rarely experience the difficulties Western women do. In the Japanese language there is not even a term for hot flashes. Asian women who adopt the Western diet also adopt Western health problems. Eastern Asian women traditionally eat soya beans, which contain natural plant hormones that can replace their own natural estrogen levels.

As menopause approaches, your body produces less estrogen, so you need to replace it, not chemically but naturally so that soy can be absorbed into your body to maintain optimum health. Of course, just a soy-rich diet is not enough on its own. But it can help produce the estrogen which you might go to the doctor for. You can buy soy in a shop and eat it as food, which may help you live a long, healthy life and bring balance and maintenance to these delicate issues of life.

I have prayed for women who were going through the change of life, and I have seen the power of God come upon them. Where one day they were having their normal menstrual cycle, the next month the cycle wasn't there any more. The women didn't even notice the change. They went straight from menstruating to a finished menopause in weeks, not years, with no hot flashes.

My wife never had any menopausal problems because we believed it wasn't the will of God for the body to function so that one would go half-crazy. I have prayed for other women, and I have seen God do the same for them. They went from a productive time to an unproductive time, from having menstrual cycles to having a healthy, beautiful life. Don't you think that sounds more like the will of God than five or so years of hot flashes and irregular blood pressure? There's got to be a better way, but satan has deceived us and said, "There is no better way. Grin and bear it." Friend, we can laugh with the joy of the Lord and do without it. God wants us to have abundant life and He wants us to have it now!

It's time to renew our minds to accept the newness of this thought: You are not made for debauchery and pain and cramps and sickness. Every one of those areas of your body that suffers pain was created for joy. Your body was made for pleasure, made for goodness, made for laughter, made to express the life of Christ, and to bring glory to His holy name.

CHAPTER FOURTEEN

Abundant What???

We had come home from one of our trips overseas. We had been to Europe, and things were not particularly happy in some of the churches we visited. We did our best and the Lord did some wonderful things, but I came home feeling very disappointed because I knew that it was possible for something else and something better to happen there. I had the house to myself as June had gone shopping.

I got into the middle of the house and the utter despondency of the whole European thing hit me. I stood there, squeezing my eyes closed, clenching my fists, screwing up my face, looking up to the heavens. I said, "Lord, I really don't believe anything too much is going to happen in those places." I had prayed hours into the night in Holland—hours and hours, day after day—and in Germany and Belgium. I prayed and believed for greater things than what I saw.

As I stood in the middle of my room, the thought of those places came to me; the pastors there, the local situations. I just couldn't see God doing the things I had believed for. In the end, with tears in my eyes, I said to the Lord, "It's almost like there's a spirit of impossibility over all of that area, the spirit of impossibility."

Chernobyl was not far away from where we had been in the city of Kiev, Ukraine, just a few miles up the road. When the nuclear power plant in Chernobyl blew up in 1986, a huge atomic cloud went across Europe. In talking to a doctor, he said that it wouldn't be long before little children and others began to come to the local medical clinics with unknown lumps, cancers, tumors, and growths of all descriptions. "Because," he said, "there's a death cloud hanging over Europe."

And as I was in my room, I felt like a death cloud was hanging over me due to the despondency of the situation. I said, "It's a spirit of impossibility over that place, Lord. I don't know how it will ever be broken. It's impossible. It's impossible to break through."

I had gone to Europe about ten years in a row. We'd ministered to people and we'd seen some great things, some great changes in those nations. New churches had been started, and it was wonderful to behold, but it was nothing compared with the need there.

I stood in my room, raised my face as tears trickled down my cheeks, and said, "It's the spirit of impossibility. Why are You sending me back there constantly when it's so hard? It's impossible, Father. It's impossible. It is just impossible. It won't happen, Father. It can't happen. It's impossible."

This went on for half- to three-quarters of an hour. Down in my spirit—way, way down deep in the inner recesses of my spirit—there was a little voice and it said, But *all things are possible to him who believes* (Mark 9:23, <u>NKJV</u>). But I was able to drown that out with my melancholy prayer to God. But the more I said, "There's a spirit of impossibility," the little voice became louder and started to move up my spirit. *All things are possible to him who believes.* "Oh, no," I said. "It won't happen. It can't happen. I've been there." And then this echo in my spirit would say, Oh, but *all things are possible to him who believes.* In the end, I was nearly screaming it out, yelling out at Him, "It's impossible! It won't happen! It won't happen!"

The voice kept coming up and coming up: "It is possible. It is possible." Then all of a sudden, the little voice met my vocal cords, and instead of my saying, "It is impossible," I was yelling out at the top of my voice, "It is possible! All things are possible to him who believes!" And all of a sudden, that spirit of heaviness just lifted off of me, and I started to jump around, because it was possible.

I began to see the possibilities of faith, the possibilities of the Word, the possibilities of the promises of God. I began to see that the possibilities of God are possible! I began to see that the situation in

Europe was possible. I began to see that those men who were pastoring those churches could have this same infusion of faith that I was enjoying—the possibilities of a great move of God. Oh, it was, indeed, possible!

I ran up and down the hallway. I lay on the floor. I kicked my feet. I was so excited. I was carried away with the exuberance of the possibilities of what God could do. The spirit of faith can do anything; the spirit of unbelief will accomplish nothing. But the goodness of God can achieve everything. The hardest person can be made as soft as clay.

The most beautiful anointing of the Spirit lay upon me and kept bubbling up out of my spirit, "It is possible. It is possible. If you believe, it is possible." The goodness of God! I ran back into the kitchen. I jumped up and down. I clapped my hands. I ran up and down the hallway again. I had not enjoyed my God so triumphantly in a long time. The possibilities of the Lord; oh, it was so exciting! It is possible to have abundant life!

Our problem is that we look for wrong answers. We look for answers out of our own poverty mentality. We try to make a great future from our past, from our knowledge, or from some past experience or vision, but it doesn't happen that way. For every new calamity, there is a new Word of God. For every new trial, there is a new understanding of the purposes of God. And for every nation, there is a direct, dynamic, explosive Word that will break through every barrier and will release the life, the Spirit, into people who are hungry to receive.

We often think that such anointing is too big for us, that we're not worthy of it. Why would God want to give it to us? Well, why wouldn't God want to give it to us? All we have to do is get ready for it.

Just as when I was saying that the situation was impossible, my spirit was saying, "But all things are possible to him who believes." And I began to see a change, not only when I went to Europe, but I began to see a change everywhere I went because I could see that change was possible. It didn't matter what the problem was; if God was on the scene, then He could change it. He has the ability just to say a word. Just one word, one sentence, can change a person's life forever. Just one message can change a church overnight. We've seen it happen on numerous occasions.

In Belgium several years ago we saw God bring about a change that was awesome. Where no churches were being built, where no churches were being opened, where people were being told by ministers that there would never be a revival or a move of God in Belgium, now they are having it. Churches are opening. I have heard people in different nations say that they're going to Belgium because God has called them to Brussels.

God is starting to do what has never been done in the history of Brussels. A word from God changed it. The change is electric, it is inspiring. People are starting to speak the Word of the Lord, and they're seeing with the eyes of vision instead of groping blindly in the dark, because God has come on the scene.

We can break the boundaries of what we see by the power of the Word of the Lord. The invisible power of the Word can come in like a two-edged sword and break through the cloud of doubt and the cloud of death that hangs over people's lives—maybe over yours—and bring a release.

For years, God had been doing some good things for me. But then, when I really looked into my thoughts and my prayers, I found I was in survival mode. We were surviving because it was a very difficult problem. Well, those are the facts of life.

You may have a difficult problem; it will either stay there and you'll maneuver yourself around it, or you'll bring some other faculties into operation that will counteract that one and you'll get by. You'll circumnavigate the problem. You'll tunnel under or you'll fly over, but the problem will just have to stay there. You hit survival mode.

Financially, you're surviving. In your spiritual life there's a little bit of Bible, a little bit of prayer, a little bit of church, and you're surviving. You don't do too much. You're not a threat to anybody. You just keep on going the way you're going: go to work, come home, feed the children, put them to bed. You do the same thing day in and day out. You love Jesus and you're so excited about some of the messages you hear, but you never change. You're just surviving.

You never get too excited. You don't get too down. You just

keep it at that level. You can handle it at that level. You're surviving. You're not a threat to anybody; you're surviving, you get by.

Solomon was one of those extravagant men in his worship to God. After opening the temple he had built, he brought so much and offered sacrifice of thousands and thousands of sheep (See I Kings 8:5). He brought an extravagant worship to the Lord. Oh, how Solomon laid it on! He wasn't in survival mode. He was exploring the future. He was sowing seed to determine the quality of the future that he wanted.

Solomon sowed worship. He worshiped God extravagantly, which twice resulted in God coming to visit and talk with him. And God asked the now-famous question, "What do you want me to give you?" And Solomon said, "Lord, I want Your wisdom. Please, give me wisdom." And because Solomon asked the right thing, God said, "I will not only make you the wisest man, but I'll make you the richest man in the world" (see I Kings 3:5-13).

So Solomon sowed his extravagant worship; his wholehearted desire to worship God with all of his heart was expressed in every shape that he gave his life. He loved his God and he wanted everybody to know how much he loved Him. And because of Solomon's actions, God couldn't stay in heaven. God was attracted, brought down into Solomon's room. God spoke to him, unraveled His greatness, and showed him His glory. And Solomon, from then on, was known as the wisest man.

People came from everywhere to see Solomon. They came into the great man's home, into his palace. They looked at the great things he had done, how he clothed his soldiers and his court attendants, the splendor in which they lived because of Solomon's great wisdom, but also because of his great worship. And on top of that, there was great wealth.

When I have a particular problem that I can't get through in my prayer—when I need something, either financial or in the realm of the Spirit—then I do something extravagant. I put more money in the offering. I sow more. I get out of bed earlier than I normally do. I spend more time waiting on God. And I go out of my way to be especially kind to somebody else, to bless somebody, to cheer them up, to do something that costs me something.

And it doesn't take long—sometimes the next day or the next week—before long there it is. I touch that anointing. I receive that thing which I need. The Lord blesses me in a new way. Verses begin to be quickened in the Word because I break through the possible into the realm of the impossible. Life becomes an adventure. It isn't dull. But if it should become dull, colorless, and boring, we smarten it up. We smarten our devotions. We change our focus. We're not going to be mediocre and fail. We want to excel for the glory of God!

CHAPTER FIFTEEN

Breaking the Poverty Curse

. . . love that is unconditional will benefit all you know and make a better you, with an environment of good words and good works so that all about us there is an atmosphere of blessing, and faith is generated out of that. It becomes an atmosphere—like the leaves of a tree—that covers us and enables us to walk in a Christ-exalting atmosphere. Enjoyment and joy will be part of that atmosphere because of the anticipation of what we are going to see today and what we are going to receive tomorrow, all because we planted seeds of goodness and faith when we blessed people yesterday. We had good thoughts yesterday; therefore, today we can reap. Tomorrow we can reap again because we're sowing good seeds today. Some seeds take a little while to harvest, but don't forget, in a little acorn there's a huge tree. Be like the man who looked at a seed and said, "I don't see a seed, I see a forest."

Every seed we sow with anticipation and faith can produce great returns, the reaping of the goodness of God. Because we sow to the Spirit, we can of the Spirit reap life. We can revel in the anticipation of what God is going to do for us tomorrow. *What are You going to do for us, Lord? How are You going to do it?* Oh, the excitement, the anticipation, the faith that is generated by sowing seed lifts our spirits so that we're able to touch an anointing in God that otherwise we would not have access to. Unbelieving, negative and critical thoughts never, ever bring great blessings.

In Acts 5, Ananias and Sapphira open up new territory for us because they gave what satan told them to give. They had made up their minds to give what they should give to God, but then satan came and infested their minds with negative believing, and satan told them what to give. They kept the part that God wanted, kept it back for themselves because the devil told them to.

How many times have you had a good thought, a God thought—not a good idea but a *God* idea? You have a God idea, you meditate on it, and then you back off of it. You get other thoughts that are lesser, easier to attain, and within the realm of possibility, so nothing very exciting ever happens. But when you have God ideas and sow God ideas, you can have a God-induced harvest. Refuse satan's ideas; they are deadly.

Unresolved conflicts can become a lump that sticks in your spirit and controls your life, unless you systematically deal with them so you can enter into the fullness of what God has for you. You can have controlling strongholds of pride, fear, bitterness, hate, revenge, anger, inferiority, and intimidation. The list is almost endless, but you need to deal with them systematically. God wants to bless you. Press into the abundance of what He has for you. Sow in goodness and mercy all the days of your life. You can reap today and continue to be a blessing as you sow what you reap. You can reap constantly; an abundant life is guaranteed for you when you do things according to the knowledge of God.

One of the contentious things that has hit the church world is the thought of prosperity. I believe there has been, in some circles, an overemphasis and a wrong emphasis on prosperity. I was one of those who treated prosperity with great caution. I was careful about how I approached it with my church and how I taught my congregation about it. It was never very positive because I was fighting an attitude of prosperity being taught in a church near us that was not really Scriptural. And so, to try to bring a balance, my teaching became negative.

I was negative in my giving and negative in my receiving. As a matter of fact, I didn't know how to receive. It was difficult for me to receive.

When my wife and I started itinerating, they'd ask us what we were expecting. We didn't know what to say because we had never been generous givers and we didn't know how to receive. Consequently, our receiving hadn't been all that grand. I started to read the Scriptures, and I began to realize that I had been missing out on one of the great areas of the Gospel of Jesus Christ. I saw the truth of the law of giving and receiving, and how God rejoices in the prosperity of His people! Why would God want us to be withdrawn, restrained, outnumbered, out-financed, or outmaneuvered?

There's never enough money in church to do things. It's full of negative people looking for help from somewhere. It's because we don't give. We haven't learned that prosperity is a blessing from God. You can interpret the word *prosperity* any way you like. But what we'd been experiencing had been just *enough*. I didn't realize that God was *more than enough*. I didn't understand, in all the years I had been a Christian, that God wanted to give me more. I wasn't believing for it, I wasn't preparing for it, I wasn't sowing for it.

When Joseph started to come into the goodness and favor of God, he had to build some big barns. He had to take down those miserable, little, faithless, fearful barns, and he had to build before the harvest came in. He had to go and get all the lumber, the tradesmen, and tell them, "Build big barns." They said, "Why, Joseph?" And he said, "I believe we're going to have a big harvest." And so he built big barns, big sheds, and big receiving yards. He trained the people on how to count the harvest as it came in and how to store it.

Scripture says that Joseph taught Pharaoh's wise men wisdom (See Genesis 41). He taught them how to contain the harvest. And so, like Joseph, I'm preparing for a full harvest. I'll open another bank account especially for the harvest I believe I'm going to receive so that I will know what God has done and so I'll know that which is God's part. And I won't keep back part. I will give God everything that He requires . . . and I'll give Him some things He doesn't require! I just want to get into His good books. And Scripture tells me that, according to the measure that I mete out, it will come back again (see Matthew 7:2). If you cast your bread upon the waters, it will come back after many days (see Ecclesiastes 11:1). I want to encourage you to sow. I want to encourage you to give to ministry.

In I Kings 17, Elijah went to the widow and said, "Give me

what you have there to eat." And she said, "I only have enough for my son and myself, and then we're going to die. The source of our supply has been cut off."

The Lord showed me in a vision that if the woman hadn't given to Elijah, she would have died. But I saw her going to her barrel of meal and oil and giving to the man of God.

When we support ministry, we give our biggest seed out of our need. The widow had a life-and-death situation, but she gave, and once she gave to the man of God, she never, ever lacked. There was always plenty to eat and enough to spare—always enough, and leftovers. She could go as often as she wanted to that barrel of meal and that cruse of oil and there was always plenty to eat. She could go ten times a day or a hundred times a day. It didn't matter, because she had sowed and given to the man of God.

I have learned to give to men and women of God—not just pay tithes, but see a ministry and give to it. Keep sowing, and give to the work of God. Look at somebody who is outside your own environment and watch what God does. The Lord showed me that to sow into another man's vineyard was pleasing to Him, so I have sowed to other people's vineyards.

It's the principle of health, of giving, of abundance. God has done more for my wife and me financially in the last two or three years than in all our lives, because we've taken it upon ourselves to sow to the ministry, to sow into other people's vineyards. And we have seen the blessing of God. We've never been happier or healthier. The blessing of the Lord is so abundant!

Here is a last word on strongholds. Have you ever wondered why so many people go on and even touch God in a great way, and then they fall away? Why is it that we're up-and-down in our Christian experience? Why is it that we cannot maintain that beautiful sense of relationship that we once had? I guess at some time or other we've all thought of this, and it breeds in us a sense that we're not favorites with God—we're not on the inside, we're not one of His special people. It makes us have a sense that we're worthless, that we lack self-worth. And it brings all sorts of ingrown problems with it. But let me tell you this: The reason we can do great, successful things is because of the yieldedness of our lives and the good things of God.

We all face times in our lives when we come against a stronghold that is of anger or of a moral nature, and that stronghold will stand there like a mountain. We can try to hit it, but we don't know how to deal with it. We become despondent, maybe go into despair. We sit back, and then we go at it again. We make a fresh dedication. We come against the stronghold—it can be opposition, self-pity, inferiority, pride, unforgiveness, bitterness—and that stronghold will start to rise up in our hearts. And instead of dealing with it, we may let it go until it grows and it becomes such a stronghold that it exalts itself against the moving of the Spirit. It's not that you are lacking self-worth, it's not that your position in Christ has changed, it's just that there's something that needs to be dealt with.

When you do deal with the stronghold and conquer it, then it doesn't have a hold on you that is strong. You've diminished its path. You can go on in peace, and there can be a greater anointing of the Spirit that comes over you and into your ministry. This is going from victory to victory, from faith to faith, from glory to glory. And the way we go on is to deal with strongholds.

When a stronghold is first formed, it is just the work of the flesh. And there are all sorts of works of the flesh that could be enumerated. These works of the flesh are the stronghold of the mind, something that we refuse to let go of and deal with. If we persist in that area of the stronghold, then there is an evil spirit that can begin to be involved in it, because it becomes the gateway through which demonic forces can begin to operate.

The majority of people don't have a demonic problem, but if we persist in bitterness, we allow the stronghold to become a fortress. We can get rid of that demonic influence by getting rid of the stronghold. Is it worthy to note that when we remove the stronghold, our position in Christ hasn't changed? God can bring us to that area so we will deal with the thing that is influencing us. If we don't deal with it, it can scar and mar our spirits, and often it will cause people to lose heart, to lose faith, and some even backslide.

The strongest Christian is as strong as the anointing upon him and as consistent as the strongholds in his life. How can great men fail? Because of strongholds they never dealt with in their young lives. How can we succeed? If we apply ourselves to wisdom, God can give us the victory. He's on our side to bless us and make us more than conquerors!

CHAPTER SIXTEEN

A Way of Escape

Sometimes we feel that the life of God is a maze. We've probably all been in a maze at one time or another. We walk around this corner, that corner, and we can become very lost. There is a way out, but we have to look for it. Sometimes we retrace our same steps, or we think of a pathway that has the attraction of being the way to get out of the maze.

If you physically have not been in a maze, you may have seen drawings of mazes, usually in cartoons and children's books. How do you find your way out of a maze and get the prize? You can draw, with your pencil, a line up and down and in and out until you find the way to the outside of the maze. Sometimes, it takes a little time because they can be very tricky.

Life can be like a maze. Sometimes the devil does it. Sometimes God allows it, because all the time the Lord is trying to show us that there are victories, but our faith has to grow to take us to the next level, to achieve the next part of God's will for us, the outworking of what we will put into the lives of others. And until we learn to get direction from God, we will walk around as if in a maze, and people will think that's the entire Christian walk. It is not the entire Christian walk. Some of the difficulties we face are because we haven't read God's Word enough, or our emotions are so low that we make crazy decisions that cause us to end up in a greater maze filled with disturbance and torment and fear.

But the Word of God in I Corinthians 10:13 says, *No temptation has overtaken you except such as is common to man: but God is faithful, Who will not allow you to be tempted beyond* [above] *what you are able, but with the temptation will also make a way of escape that you may be able to bear it.* So, when every temptation or trial comes our way, there is a segment of hope. There is a doorway for escape. There is an answer to alleviate the pressure, to alleviate the pain. God can show us what that is, and that gives us hope.

God can give you hope. He can give you encouragement. He can speak a word to you. You may have a dream in the night, or He might quicken a Scripture to you that is the answer, the key, to the present situation in which you find yourself. It is there and it's a revelation to your heart. You take that word and use it against your temptation. You can take the inspiration that you get from God—that verse of Scripture—and use it to give you victory and maintain it.

In Judges 15:14-20 is the story of Samson and how he defeated the enemy—a thousand Philistines—with the jawbone of an ass. After the battle, he was very thirsty—who wouldn't be thirsty after a fight like that? He was bone-dry and he said to the Lord, "I'm dying of thirst. What am I going to do?" The Lord said, "Go to the place of your victory and I will make a hole in the jawbone of the ass and I will give you water to drink."

There's much discussion as to whether Samson went to the place, and God dug a well in the ground, or if there was a place in the jawbone of the ass that God hollowed out to give him some natural water. The point of the story is that he went to the place of his *victory*, not the place of defeat or failure. And when he got there, there was God's provision of water. He was able to satisfy his thirst and he felt great.

Someone once prophesied over me that I would go to my place of victory; I would need divine enablement and strength, and I would get it at the place of my victory. I was told that God would hollow the jawbone of the ass for me to have refreshment and to renew my strength. The prophecy gave me hope. I knew there was hope, I knew there would be a way out of any coming problem, whatever it might be. But I didn't know how to apply the prophecy. How could I apply it? The practicality of it was that I didn't have a jawbone, except for the one in my face, and I didn't have any implements of warfare, because I walked where it is not carnal but mighty through God to the pulling down of strongholds. So, where was I going to get this drink that would enable me to be replenished after I had ministered to hundreds of people?

One day, feeling famished and weak, I had a drink of water — two glasses of water. Then I had a third. I could feel my strength coming back. And it was almost as if, as I drank the natural water, that my spirit was partaking and drinking at the fountain that never runs dry. There was a spiritual enabling as I did a natural thing. Now when I feel spiritually famished or dry, I make sure that I—almost ceremoniously—go to the faucet, turn it on, and drink one or two glasses of water. As I do this, I praise God in my heart and, almost without fail, I gain spiritual stamina and spiritual strength. You might want to try it sometime.

Look for your hope in your problem. Look for the way out because there's no escape if you try to run away from it. But there is a key that God can give you in your moment of despair that can get you out of the difficulty, a key that will break its back, that can cause power to flood into your heart and enable you to bear it. Inner strength is renewed by an anointing of the refreshing glory of God in your spirit.

Remember the story of Jeremiah when he was thrown into the pit? When it came time for him to come out of the pit one of the servants threw down some rags to put under his armpits so he wouldn't tear his flesh as they dragged him up out of the pit (See Jeremiah 38:10-12). Sometimes, in time of despair, God will throw down some rags of hope to you to cushion the load. It can help the journey out of your pit as you learn to praise Him and love Him and to know that this is for your good.

There is a secret place of the Most High. And as we come into the secret place of the Most High—not when we come out, but when we come into the secret place—that's when we have an intimate relationship with the Lord.

In Isaiah 45:3, while talking to Cyrus, God says that there are *hidden riches of secret places* that God is going to give him. When you come into temptations or trials that look as if they're going to break your back, there is a ray of light. You're in this experience because there are treasures that are placed for you in the darkness. As you yield to the place of God and allow Him to minister to you, you can discover the treasures of darkness. The Holy Spirit can overshadow you and implant treasures of darkness, hidden riches that alone are discovered in the secret place. You have to go into the secret place to be alone with Him, to allow the ministry of the Spirit and the hand of the Lord to be with you in that time, and you're never there alone. He is right there so that the spirit and the temptation, whatever it may be, is never too strong for you. When people say, "I can't cope," I believe they are wanting out. You can cope. His grace is sufficient and He is there, always, to bless you and to help you through this particular area of life that you're in.

This Man is the Lord who is there. This Man is also *El Shaddai,* which means "the breasted one." So, it appears that God has some semblance of a breast, for nurturing, for caring, for mothering.

CHAPTER SEVENTEEN

The Mystery of Healing

When it comes to healing, there are many mysteries. Why is it that good people are sometimes not healed, yet some people, not even believing to be healed, have the power of God come through their bodies and they are healed? There are some things we are unable to understand. And yet, there is healing for us. There is the covenant of healing. In Exodus 15:26, God told Moses, *I am the Lord that healeth thee.* We have a covenant that God makes with us when we are born again: we are to receive healing because He is the Lord who heals.

When we come into intimacy, fellowship, and worship with the Lord, we can ask and believe to receive healing because of our covenantal rights. We must renew our minds to this, because generally, we find fault with the fact that many are not healed. We need to believe that healing is ours, that it has been purchased for us on the Cross, and that the Lord delights to heal us.

There is the promise of healing in I Peter 2:24, *by His stripes [we] were healed.* God promised to heal us; in fact, we were healed when He died on the Cross for us. So the provision for healing is there. Our bodies can be made normal, to function according to the Master Designer's plan. He has a blueprint for our lives and He knows all of our parts. Therefore, He can heal us and make us whole. We can believe to receive healing because it is a promise; a promise made to us in the Old Testament in Isaiah 53:4, 5, and a promise made to us in the New Testament that what He suffered in His body atones for us and brings us to wholeness (See I Peter 2:24).

Believe it in your mind, think about it, think of the possibilities of divine health, the anointing, and the expectancy that comes with it. Believe to see a difference in your mobility and in your bodily functions that sometimes are not in line with normal living. Believe God is going to heal them. Expect a miracle in those areas of your life. If it's pain or any other feminine difficulty, it's not yours; you don't have to suffer it, you don't have to have it. The promise of the Lord is to break every curse, so believe for health and wellbeing.

The law of *gifts of healings* is found in I Corinthians 12:9. There are *gifts of healings*—"gifts" is plural and "healings" is plural. There are different types of healings for different types of sicknesses. And it seems that God has covered the whole spectrum of sickness—inadequacies, pain, sorrow, grief, biological defenses, and diseases that we pick up along the way.

As Dr. Margaret Smith has said, "A lot of our difficulties are because of our mental approach to things because of negativity and the acceptance of a lower level of living because we don't know any better. But as we accept that there is a higher way, our expectancy level reaches a new dimension that releases life into our whole body."

That helps explain the woman with the issue of blood who was mentioned in Matthew 9. It wasn't the gifts of healings, nor the covenant, nor the promise that brought her healing, but she said in her heart, *If I can touch the hem of His garment, I will be made whole* (see v. 21). I don't know where on earth she ever got the concept of touching the hem of Jesus' garment. Who told her that? What ingenious thought allowed her mind to think that she could touch the hem of His garment and be healed? Maybe she thought that because of the type of disease she had, the rest of the people wouldn't accept it, or she was embarrassed to come to the Lord, or she didn't want to worry the Master.

But she repeated the words to herself all the time. She thought about it and dreamed about it, she ate it, drank it, slept it. *If only I may touch His garment, I shall be made well.* She talked herself into a healing. She didn't let the disease that she'd had for twelve years talk her out of her healing.

Being the woman that she was, she would have known that in the book of Deuteronomy, there is the promise of healing (see Deuteronomy 32:39), and in Psalm 103:2, it says that He *healeth all* [our] *diseases*. I don't know if these Scriptures were in her mind. She didn't have any right to touch the hem of His garment, except that it was what she said within her heart. It was her motivation. It brought her faith to the surface, and off she went.

To touch the hem of His garment, she had to get on her hands and knees. Mark 5:27 says that she pushed through the people who were gathered together and clamoring for Jesus. Possibly, she could have grazed her hands or her shoulders, but she went to the ground and she touched the hem. As her faith touched the hem of His garment, she drew the virtue of Christ into her own body (see v. 30). The life of Christ came and corrected—instantly—the problem. She probably felt the power of God working in her body, and then the fire of the Holy Ghost adjusting her womb, drying out her bleeding problem, and causing her body to be well. She would have felt excited as the power of God surged through her body.

Before she got there, Jesus didn't know anything about her. He was ministering to all those people, but they were just wanting healing; they didn't have faith. Then this woman came, touched His garment, and He said, *Who touched me?* And the disciples said, "Well, everybody's touching you." "Oh, no," He said, "there's a special hand that touched me. Faith touched me, and virtue went into her" (see Luke 8:45, 46).

I don't know if I have the right to say this or not, but because of this story, I feel there is a special anointing for women to be healed, because the Bible says, *virtue [went] out of Him* (v. 46). You can call it life, you can call it what you like, but it's virtue. It's the ability to quench the problem, to adjust the problem, to bring healing, life, and expectancy. This is exciting!

When I'm praying for ladies around the world, I ask God, "Lord, release the healing virtue for women." And I believe there's healing virtue for women now. And if there is, I'm going to make it widely known, rather than isolating it for this story: There's healing virtue for women.

Jesus was happy to be identified with this woman and with her disease. God is happy to be identified with you and your feminine problem. He is happy to release His life into your body, into the intimate, personal parts of your body, and heal them. It was His majestic hand that created them, and He has maintenance power to bring them back to the design that was patented long ago.

Every woman should be encouraged to press in, to touch by faith the hem of His garment. The covenant is there, the promise is there, the gifts are there, and your faith is there. Believe that your feminine disabilities are going to clear up and healing is going to come in great measure.

I'm going to do something in this book that's pretty unusual. I have traced a copy of my hand—my hand is not any better than anybody else's—and I'm going to put it in the book (page 158). I want you to be able to put your hand on that place where I've laid my hand. There are going to be a lot of copies of this book published, but I'm going to believe that when I lay my hand on it, that the virtue of the healing gift will flow from this page to every other page. And when you put your hand on it or lay it on your body, we're going to believe together that this page is a point of contact, and that virtue can be released.

A friend of mine in the United States was very, very sick. We had prayer but he didn't, in any way, become better. I was praying one day and the Lord said, "Send him a faxed copy of your hand." I prayed over this for days, and to everybody who came into the house I said, "Lay your hand on this spot here." So, they laid their hands on the drawing of my hand, and we faxed it all the way to the United States. The man got it, laid it on his chest, put it under his pillow, and he began to get better. Later he told me that the drawing of my hand was the turning point. He was still on some medication, but he got better.

That was the turning point. I laughed and said, "What did you do with it then, throw it in the trash?" He said, "Oh, no, I've got it filed away. I will never forget the day they brought in the drawing of your hand."

I was excited by that and I want you to be excited about this. You can turn back the pages of the book, you can lay it on your body, or lay your hand upon it, and it can become a point of contact for you. It's a place you can release your faith. It is the place that you can say, "God met me at this point"—the point of your need, the point of your release of faith. It can be the point of life for you.

Remember Paul; there were handkerchiefs and aprons that went from his body and brought healing, and demons left (see Acts 19:11, 12). It was a transference of anointing into a cloth, and there is a transference of anointing into this page. We have seen a lot of people helped with the praying for handkerchiefs, and we've got to put this in. It's going to be different and their account will be different because I'm expecting great things. I want you to be healed and to live a life with quality. I call it the healing virtue that flows into your body. In Jesus' Name, receive that healing virtue, in the Name of Jesus.

In the book of Acts it says that Peter went down the street, and his shadow healed the people. They brought people out on beds and on their couches, they brought them from miles and miles around, and as his shadow passed over them, they were healed. Demons left, and it says they were all healed (see Acts 5:14-16).

What was the virtue of the shadow of Peter? I believe it wasn't just a shadow. I believe it was the manifestation of the glory of God upon him, that as the people lay in the streets and he walked among them, the transference of the glorious power of God touched the people, and multitudes were healed. The healing ministry of Peter is underestimated and underrated. How long was this manifestation of God's healing power upon him? There were possibly hundreds of thousands of people, and he healed them as he walked up and down the street.

Like those waiting for Peter to pass by, believe to receive the goodness of God. God is good all the time; His mercy endures forever (see I Chronicles 16:34). We come to the throne of grace to receive mercy and, at times, grace to help in time of need. The blessing of the Lord is on you to bring you into health and His blessing. Renew your mind to it, confess it, pray it, and thank Him for it daily. And give God a chance to bring His lovely role of grace to pass in your body, which is the temple of the Holy Spirit.

I believe there is a new dimension of the healing gifts that God is beginning to pour out upon us. We are going to see the spectacular parts of the healing ministry of Jesus. There has been great opposition to the supernatural. People don't like it. They preach about it, talk about it, and write about it.

I am sure we can agree that there have been things said and done that have marred the body of Christ. But that doesn't take away from the reality that God is *the same yesterday, today, and forever* (Hebrews 13:8, NKJV). Jesus is the healing Savior and He wants to move upon us and touch us tremendously.

I believe with all my heart that there is a move now, as the intercessors who are leading us believe, that the demonic opposition—the satanic opposition against the power of God—will be broken down because we are going to move more and more into the supernatural realm of our lives. There is so much trouble on every hand, and trouble is not the lord of our life; Jesus is. In His peace and His life and power we can come to depend upon Him entirely and we can see greater things coming to pass. But let the intercessors pray. Let them pray against the spirits of infirmity that cause deforming things to happen to people, and let them pray that the diseases that take life will be deaf and dumb, in the Name of Jesus.

Believe to see the glory of God. I believe to see it, and I want you to believe to see it. We're going to come into this transforming, miracle-working power more today than we've seen in the last twenty-four years. *This is the day which the Lord hath made; we will rejoice and be glad in it* (Psalm 118:24). Claim your healing, believe for it, receive it today, in Jesus' Name!

CHAPTER EIGHTEEN

Your Body—The Temple

There are four seasons: summer, autumn, winter, and spring. The summer of your life are days you have successes. God is there. God blesses you with His fruitfulness, like when a tree blossoms and has fruit that is easy to pick and come into your hands. A ministry can be like that and life can be like that. Everything's working well.

But then autumn, or fall, comes. The leaves fall off the trees, and it's not long before there is no more fruit. The clouds over us are dark. It's raining, it's wet, it's blustery, and it's cold, and we're discouraged. Life can be like that. Perhaps no one calls you on the phone. Your children are not around; there are no friends. All of a sudden, everything is difficult and different. There's not the fruitfulness there once was.

You are transitioning. You're going from last year's blessing, last year's walk with God, last year's intimacy with Him, all the good things that were there, and you're going through a period of transitioning from summer to winter. But you have to go through fall first.

We haven't always understood fall. We just think that it's a time of bleakness, but it is actually a time when a tree is being reestablished. In the fall, its roots go down because the tree doesn't have to surge life up into the limbs and the leaves. The roots go down looking for fresh nourishment, for new sources of water. And the tree puts out roots. When the winds blow one way upon it, the tree stretches out the roots in the other direction to keep it in balance.

This is what God expects of us. When these times of transitioning come, we go from one prophetic revelation to another prophetic season, a season when God wants to do new things, to touch new people, and to do new things in us. It means that we go from the old to the new, but we can't bring the old over. All the leaves have to come off. There's no fruit on us anymore because the fruit is out on the limb, at the end of the limb.

We have to learn to stretch out and reach into the future because it is during this time of autumn when God gives us our word, our new prayers, and our new faith. But difficulties can come at this time. We have a predator that lurks in the dark, waiting for us to fail. And it's in this period of time that we often sense failure. It's a time when we feel the sickest. Our headaches rage, our friends don't call, and no one is interested in us. We want a friend, but no one has time for us. It is a time when we have to press into God. It is a time requiring great faithfulness, because nothing is happening. There's no finance about. It's like a wilderness we've come into.

But, it's all the planning of God, because our spiritual roots are going down into maturity. We're being established in the present truth, and we're absorbing the presence of God and the Word of the Lord for our future. This is when He's birthing within us the Word for the future.

This is often a time of repentance, of reconsecration, of rededication, of going through our life and taking stock to see exactly where we are. Our problems are highlighted. We become self-conscious; not necessarily self-centered, but self-conscious. We're conscious of our needs and our problems, and they're the same as everybody else's. There may be a "Job's comforter" who comes along and tells us what to do, and then hurts us like anything. They say the wrong thing at the right time and it crucifies us again. But it's only the flesh that gets hurt, and it's good for us. It's good for us to receive these wounds of a friend who is faithful.

We reassess our vision and our goal during this period of seeming loneliness—the autumn of our experience. If we are wise during this time, we will fast and pray and allow God to work His purposes in our hearts and keep focused on Him. This is when He can start to give us a word that will help our future. But we can't look back and bring lesser mentality into the present day because we've never lived tomorrow. We need tomorrow's bread, tomorrow's vision, tomorrow's motivation, and we can get it today. What we say and what we sow today, we'll reap tomorrow.

Do you want flowers in your garden next month? Then you prepare the ground, and you sow the seed today. You water it, then you walk away, leave it, and let the seeds do their job. They will be down in the soil, bursting with life, and you won't be able to see anything. But the seeds are down there. Then, the seeds shoot up their little thin fingers in praise to God, and they grow and blossom.

Sometimes during the winter, the seeds are still in the soil, yet the cold, adverse weather doesn't kill them. They just maintain their place, ready to spring forth when the season is right. When the prophetic season is released, when the Son of Righteousness shines upon us, the blessing and power of God can become manifest. The winter has a great work to perform in our lives.

In Hebrews 4:13 it says, *All things are naked and open* [before] *the eyes of Him to whom we must give account.* We can't hide anything from God because everything is naked and exposed before Him. Our walk with God is so transparent that when we come into some experiences of the winter, we lose our covering, our shade, our evident, manifest life to be on our own. The loneliness of that time! I want to emphasize sufficiently that winter is a season of God for maturity, a time for maturing and coming to a place of stability with the Lord. And during that time of exposure and nakedness, God can take things off of us. The Bible says that "the Lord lifted his hand off Amaziah so he could see what was in his heart."

We sometimes forget what manner of man we are, and the Lord takes us into a winter season so we can see our heart, so we can see that it is time for another development. Change must take place, but it doesn't take place all at once. Change takes place as a process. We don't get old in ten minutes; it takes eighty years to become 80 years of age.

So the processes of life—purity, holiness—do not happen instantly. We need to go into the plateaus of life where we level off, where God can deal with us, take things out, and put things in. Then we go on to the springtime and summertime of our experiences.

Once we were flying into New York in the wintertime. I said to my wife as I looked out of the plane, "I don't know what is happening down there, but it looks like a lot of sticks sticking up out of the ground." I couldn't make it out for a long time. As we came into the airport, all of a sudden it dawned on me what it was as we got closer. The trees were without their leaves, and they looked like a lot of big sticks sticking out of the ground. Everything was exposed.

One time I had a nasty experience that turned out to be a fantastic time in the presence of the Lord. I went to my place of prayer, and the Lord spoke very clearly to me from Hebrews 4:13 which says, *All things are naked and open* [before] *the eyes of him with whom we have to do.* I didn't really appreciate that verse very early in the morning.

I closed the door and the light was off, and I felt that the Lord wanted me to stand naked in His presence. I said, "Lord, I am naked in Your presence." But he kept on pushing that verse into my heart. So, gradually, I stood naked in His presence. I was so embarrassed. I've never been more ashamed in my life. I was afraid to move because I knew that I was standing before the eyes of God. I was standing in His presence. I'd been naked before—every day when I shower, getting ready for bed, and getting up in the morning. It was no big deal. But here I was in the presence of God, and that was a big, awesome presence. He was there, and there I was, naked.

The lights were off; the room was in total blackness. There was no light coming from outside or inside. Yet, I knew I was standing before the Lord, and I felt so embarrassed. I stood there for an hour. I was too ashamed to move. Shame gripped my heart. From the crown of my head to the soles of my feet, I felt shame over all the parts of my body. I was glad when my time of prayer finished. I got my clothes on and got out of that place.

So the next morning when I came to prayer, the same thing happened. The same verse, *Everything is naked and open before the eyes of Him with whom we have to do.* I tried to pray, but I asked, "Lord, why are You demanding this? What's going on? Does it matter if I pray clothed or unclothed?" The embarrassment that was in my mind and my heart! I sat there and said, "Don't let those angels look at me."

What was happening? I was so confused, but I endeavored to pray. On the third morning, I said to the Lord—because the same thing had happened—"Lord, I have no understanding, and I'm so ashamed of myself. I'm so ashamed of my body. Please, will You wash me in the blood of Jesus and take the shame out of my heart, out of my mind, and out of my body?" I didn't understand that I was ashamed of my nakedness and ashamed of my humanity, my manhood. I asked the Lord to bring healing to my spirit.

The fourth morning it happened again. But this time I was not ashamed. I was so happy. I was rejoicing, and I didn't care if God looked at my body or not. He created it anyway, and there's nothing about my body that I am ashamed of. My body is the temple of the Holy Spirit. Every part is dedicated and holy to Him. I rejoiced that morning. It didn't bother me. I was almost sorry when the time came to stop praying.

By the fifth morning, I was prepared for something different, something better. I took with me a jug of juice, a package of cookies, and some oil. I went in and said, "Lord, I'm not ashamed of my body anymore. I open my heart; I open my mind. Take everything out that has ever offended You, or man, or me, and cleanse me, purify me. Let the fire of God touch me. Wash the fingerprints of others off of me, every laying on of hands that was not of You. Wipe the unclean influences off of me."

I dedicated and committed myself to the Lord that day. Then I got the oil and poured it on my head, more than I would normally do. I said, "Anoint my head with oil as Psalm 23 says." I put my hand on the oil. I anointed my eyes with oil and my head with oil. Then I anointed my forehead, my thinking capacities. I wanted the anointing on my mind. I anointed my eyes so I might have anointed seeing—I wouldn't look at what God didn't want me to look at, but I would see everything that He wanted me to see, naturally and in the realm of the Holy Ghost. I anointed my nose with hope of discerning the ways of God. I anointed my face. I anointed my tongue that I would speak the things of the Spirit, that He would put a guard over my mouth so I would speak righteousness.

I anointed my shoulders because the government is upon His shoulders (see Isaiah 9:6). As the body of Christ, He made our shoulders to be anointed. I anointed my heart and my chest that carries the burden and weight of the responsibility of the work of the Lord, of my family. I anointed my stomach with oil in the Name of the Lord, that all my body would be healed, and it would know the blessing and the power of God. I anointed my back. I anointed every part of my body with oil, that everything would be used to the blessing and glory of God.

I anointed my knees, that I would walk uprightly; my legs, that I would stand uprightly in the presence of the Lord. I anointed my feet with oil, that they would not be swift to shed blood but that they would walk in the ways of the Lord. That I would trample on the feet, with oil, the head of the enemy. I anointed the soles of my feet, my arms, and my hands. I bathed my hands in oil and rubbed it in.

I stood there in the presence of God, anointed as best as I could be anointed. I was covered in oil. I didn't spare the oil; I was absolutely smothered in the oil. Then I said to the Lord, *Everything is 'naked and open' before 'the eyes of Him with whom [I] have to do,* but everything that You see is dedicated and holy and committed that Your name may be glorified, because my body and every part of my body is the temple of the Holy Ghost."

Then I took Communion. I got the cookies and said, "Lord, I'm going to assimilate these to represent Your body, and I'm going to assimilate it into my body." And I had Communion, the greatest Communion that I've ever had in my life. I didn't have one tiny, little cookie, I had many cookies. I ate and consumed His life, His purity, His power, and His health.

Then I drank the juice. It wasn't a little glass; it was glass after glass. I consumed it, the blood of the covenant. That day I made a covenant with God to walk upright. Not for a day, not for a month, not for a year, but permanently, an everlasting covenant. My, how I enjoyed that juice as I drank, as it were, the blood of the Lord Jesus Christ. Every part of my life—body, soul, and spirit—was anointed, consecrated, and dedicated to the Lord.

How I enjoyed the presence of God that day! It was a day like I had never, ever had. I wasn't ashamed nor was I afraid. The Lord took my shame, and He took my fear. There was a linking, as it were, in the Spirit with the Lord that day that I'd never enjoyed before. It was deeper and sweeter. It was almost like a tryst; He committed Himself to me and I to Him that day, in a depth that we'd never had before.

As I write that, I think of all the wonderful things He's done for me, to me, and through me in days gone by. But today is a different day because there's a different commitment. And that day is sewn into my heart. There was such a consciousness of His presence, such an awareness of His truth and the confidence that I'd lacked in my life. I knew that I was His and He was mine, and His banner over me was love.

I went from that room to a conference. The power of God that flowed from that place! Maybe I shouldn't have, but I told the people at the conference the story, and how they laughed! They now call it "Frank's pornographic sermon." But it wasn't pornographic to me. It was the sweetest, deepest, most awesome covenantal day that I've ever had.

Whenever I come to a winter time in my life, I now know what to do. Winter, it is time for the shedding of leaves. There isn't much fruitfulness in this time of preparation, so that's when I go before the Lord again and stand in His presence, reaffirming a covenantal relationship (see Hebrews 4:13). I lie before the Lord, stand in His presence, sit in His presence, and assimilate His goodness—not just as a spiritual exercise, but assimilating the power and the blessing of the Lord into every part of my being.

God doesn't just speak to your spirit; He touches your body. You can feel the anointing in all of your body—in any part of your body because your body is His. He's the Lord of your body and your body is the Lord's, so why shouldn't it be healed? Why shouldn't it be well? Why should it be tormented or broken? Why should it be wounded and limp? Why should you have times of great sickness if you are yielded and committed and loving Him? The healing health and virtue of His presence—the virtue from His garment—covers you, mantles you, and impregnates you. The union and the unity is intimate and precious.

You come out of your winter into the full bloom, the full

manifestation of what He's planted within you. The assimilation that you've gone through in the winter starts to blossom and bloom in the bright sunlight of spring. You don't tell anybody what happened in the secret place of the Most High—that's a secret between the Lord and you.

The Lord said to Cyrus in Isaiah 45:3, <u>NKJV,</u> that He would give him *the hidden riches of secret places.* God has hidden riches for us. He has treasures of darkness, treasures to be opened up by His Word. And in the most trying and difficult times of our lives, if we will look to the Lord through our tears to worship and praise Him, then when the clouds are gone, we can be better men and women. We can stand and take our places, and have something to say that no one has ever heard before, the things that He's whispered—the secrets—the unraveling of mysteries, the understanding of His wisdom that must pass on His goodness to others. We've gleaned it because we were prepared to pay the price of going through all the seasons of God.

People enjoy the prophetic season when the fruit is there, the lovely, luscious, beautiful fruits of the Spirit, the graces of God that flow from our lives and touch others.

What a privilege and honor it is to have the Spirit ministering to you, blessing you, and loving you. There is no greater joy, but sometimes it comes in the winter—cold, naked, and alone. But Moses went up the mountain alone with God. (See Exodus 24:12). Ezekiel had his greatest revelations while he was alone with God. Jacob, who spent all night alone, had dreams and visions when the angels of the Lord ministered to him (see Genesis 28:11, 12). And as the shepherds watched their flocks at night, the Spirit of God came upon them and they heard the angels singing (see Luke 2:8-14).

So the nighttime—the winter—is not a time for sadness and weeping; it's a time of pressing into the presence of God and letting Him minister to you.

CHAPTER NINETEEN

The Blessing of Darkness

I had a very unusual experience. I had put my back out, and for four months I wasn't able to get relief, no matter what I did. I'd go to bed every night and get comfortable, then once I got to sleep—and I wriggled some—I would wake up with my back aching like anything. I hated the night because it was the time of pain. I'd struggle through the day, but when evening came, it was very difficult. I went to chiropractors. I even went to a hospital and had an epidural, but that didn't help. I couldn't sleep. I took pillows and a mattress and slept on the floor. Then that didn't help. I would walk around the place. I'd try to sit. The pain got worse, and it was just terrible. I became not just tired but exhausted, exhausted because I couldn't sleep.

One day I found that if I leaned against the wall and crossed my legs, I had relief from the pain. I tried to even sleep standing up against the wall. That wasn't very successful, but the pain was alleviated. I spent a lot of this time praying. I would pray for people and pray for the blessing of the Lord upon my church.

One night when I was in that position, so tired, the agony of my back was just too much. As I prayed I said, "Lord, just one touch of Your finger right onto this spot will bring healing. Why don't You heal me, Jesus? Come and heal me. Please come and heal me." I was so desperate. I waited another hour or so and nothing happened. Then I said, "Well, Lord, I am so lonely. I spend so many hours of the night awake, and I'm lonely. Everybody else is asleep and I'm so lonely. Jesus, why don't You come and comfort me? Come and keep me company, Jesus."

Tears ran down my face because I wanted someone to stand with me in the night season. I heard the outer door of our patio open. I wondered who it was because I knew everybody was in bed. Then the inner door to the room where I was standing opened, and in came Jesus. He leaned against the wall, similar to the position in which I was leaning against the wall. I could hardly handle it—there He was! I said, "Hello, Jesus," and He smiled and said, "Hello." I said, "What are You doing here?" He said, "You asked Me to come and keep you company for a while. So I've come to keep you company."

I can't remember anything that we talked about that day. It was as if the Lord eradicated it out of my mind because it wasn't important for any other occasion but for that occasion. We stood, we talked, and we shared, and He talked with me and He smiled. As I'm writing this I can still see Him: the smile on His face, the movement of His hands as He gestured while He was speaking. I know I laughed at some of the things that were said as we shared.

Then He stood up straight and I knew it was over. He smiled, and I smiled back. He turned around, walked out of the door, closed it, walked across the patio, opened the door, went out, and was gone. And I couldn't have cared less about my aching back because I'd had a visit from the Lord! He is such a comforter. Why didn't He heal me? That's another story. But in the winter, in the secret place, there are treasures of darkness.

I've always wanted to hear His heart. He wants to plant the secret things into your spirit. There is no doubt in my mind that some of the things that have come to light in the later years of my experience were sown by Him as He talked with me on that night. How long does it last? I don't know. It just seemed to last a long time, a long time.

Jesus walks with us and talks with us. He is very, very interested in us. Soon after my experience that night, the Lord spoke to me. He didn't come to me but He spoke. He told me what to do about one of the ministers in our city whom I needed to restore because he had fallen into sin. It was time for restoration. The Lord used that time. It was as if I had to come to a place of obedience.

Soon after that I met a fellow who was able to just manipulate my back a little bit, and I have had no pain in my back in all these years.

It was a season, a winter. But, oh, how fantastic it was as the days went by!

CHAPTER TWENTY

The Key to Release

Before the final chapters, I think it would be good to look again at what I've written concerning what others have done to us. We should forgive them. Forgiveness will release us and them.

If you have had an abortion, you need to repent for the murder, and the fact that your body has been subjected to this sinful practice. Ask God to make you whole because your body is the temple of the Holy Spirit.

If you have been sinned against by incest or rape or any form of molestation, forgive the person involved. Bless them in the Name of Jesus. Ask that their influence be broken off your life, including any form of immorality. Release the influence of that person's personality on you. The cleansing power of the blood of Christ can make you totally free from anything that could hinder you, free from any curses that have been put upon you by other people, by your culture, or by your race.

Any oath that has been taken needs to be broken. If there are vows you made that you don't have the ability to fulfill, ask the Lord to release you from them, along with pledges and oaths of other orders, of other societies. Any promises that you've made that you can't fulfill—maybe in your unsaved days—take it all to the blood of Jesus so He can release you from the sins of the past, from the shames of the past. Come into release in your spirit, your mind, and your body.

There's a law of association. We become like people we associate with; therefore, I don't associate with criminals, and I don't associate constantly with people who are living in an unholy manner or speaking negatively all the time. The law of association can cause that to rub off on us. Even Lot, Abraham's nephew, had his spirit, his soul, vexed by the unrighteous conversation of the Sodomites. He lost his family because of the law of association (See Genesis 19).

What you allow, you will come under. You can't allow the works of evil. In your mind, you can't meditate on them. The Scripture says not to learn the ways of the heathen (see Jeremiah 12:16, 17). Be careful of what you bring into your heart and into your mind, because your body is the temple of the living God.

The Cross of Jesus Christ, His death, burial, and resurrection must be central to everything we believe. Whatever is in the past is nailed to the Cross, and the power of the blood of Jesus Christ can break the influence of the past off us. Our sins can be forgiven, but sometimes the influence lingers. We need to eradicate that influence with the cleansing power of the blood of Jesus Christ. On the Cross Jesus Christ bore our sin, our sickness, our death, our poverty, our rejection, our disease, our sadness, our sorrow, our grief, our pain, our anxiety, our fear, our punishment, our despising, our shame, our curse, our infirmity. Jesus Christ bore our iniquities—everything that satan has invented to bring us down and to mar the image of Christ in us. Jesus Christ came to take us into His presence and to remove all the influences and marks of shame and sin.

Jesus Christ came to give us life, health, acceptance, peace, joy, blessings, abundance, grace, glory, salvation, and heaven. He came to make us whole. Whatever is in our family line, or whatever the devil's plan is for our lives, we must break its power. It cannot have influence over us. We're bought with a price; therefore, we are to glorify God in our spirits and our bodies, which are God's. We are men and women of the covenant. God has made a covenant with us.

No matter what your lot in life is now, never give up. Never, never, ever give up. Have you ever had the quits? I've wanted to quit more times than I've wanted to go on. Often I've just felt inadequate. We all feel inadequate sometimes. There are times of frustration when you can't see your way out, but never quit.

The thing that has kept me going is that I didn't want to fail Jesus. I want to see Him when my life is finished, and whatever hell I'm going through at the moment is not going to stop me. The other thought is that I don't want the devil to win this fight. Those two thoughts keep me going through the darkest hour. I have gone on relentlessly, even when I've wanted to quit. I'd tell my wife, "I'm going to quit," and she'd tell me, "I heard that yesterday."

So day by day, get through each day by praising the Lord and blessing the Lord, by clapping and rejoicing. Do some act of faith. Say something positive, not something negative. Proclaim, "I love You, Jesus. I'm not going to fail You. I'm not going to sin with my mouth." Go over the top. You'll get through it. Tomorrow can be a better day. The sun will shine. The blessing of the Lord can come. Our darkest hour is often the moment of our greatest victory. We are where we are because we keep on going back.

There is no other name under heaven given to men whereby we can be saved—no other name but the Name of Jesus. No other power but the power of Jesus. No other way but by the blood of the Lord Jesus Christ. Thank Him for the Cross. Thank Him for the power of the Cross, where the sins of the world were nailed when He died for us. His blood trickled down the Cross and has affected every generation. Worlds may come and worlds may go, leaders may rise and leaders may fall; but the blood of Jesus Christ still cleanses us from all our sin! The Gospel is still the power of God unto salvation. Put your faith in it. It can make your night into day. It can make the day a brilliant time of the blessing of the Lord.

Renew your mind. Keep thinking of the positive things that God has promised you, and you'll find that this can begin to have an effect upon your body. And when the cycles of life come, keep believing for good things. Say, "Good things are going to happen to me. Good things!"

We sow good into the Spirit, and we bring the blessing of God down. We bring the healing of God into our spirits. We open our hearts and we drink in the power of the Holy Spirit. We drink it in like the air we breathe. Breathe in the goodness of God. Breathe in the blessing of God. Breathe in His power.

Assimilate into your personality and life the life of Christ. Declare, "I'm going to be like Christ." Declare that Christ lives within you. Declare it. Say it. Believe it. Think it. Christ. Christ. Christ.

Begin to think of the miracle-working power of God. Miracles. Miracles. Miracles. The more you say it, the more opportunity it has to happen. You can affect people's lives, your life, and your family when you say, "I believe in miracles. I believe in visions. I believe in dreams. I believe in the supernatural."

The Bible is a supernatural book. We can have things that are supernatural happen to us. The only things God does are supernatural things, miraculous things, and He's waiting for us to believe. He's looking for an avenue through which He can pour His glory and His power. Do it. Do it. Do it. Do it. Do it.

There's a firm called Nike®. Its logo is on shoes, on hats, on sweatshirts—it's everywhere! Nike has a catch phrase or slogan, which is "Just do it." The word *Nike* means "man's winner" in Greek. Nike signs up successful athletes all over the world and pays them to wear its gear because these men and women are already winners, and Nike wants its products to be on winners.

"Just do it." That's the catch phrase of people who say, "We're going to do it. We're going to be faster. We're going to jump higher. We're going to achieve better. We're going to be winners. We're going to 'Just do it.'"

God wants us to do it, to be overcomers. We *can* do it. We *can* make it. We have the power of God at our disposal! The ability of the Holy Ghost is in us and is anointing us to achieve higher goals. Believe for healing to be released in your body, for your glands and everything that may not be functioning. Lay your hands on your body and command it to work according to the Master Designer's plan. We can do it. First John 4:4 says, *greater is he that is in you.* God is greater than sickness. He is greater than disease. Greater than pain is the loving power of God!

CHAPTER TWENTY-ONE

Stronghold or Stranglehold?

Second Corinthians 10:4, 5, <u>NKJV</u>, says, *For the weapons of our warfare are not carnal but mighty in God for pulling down strongholds, casting down arguments and every high thing that exalts itself against the knowledge of God, bringing every thought into captivity to the obedience of Christ.*

Strongholds are contentious thoughts that are in opposition to God's words and ways. These thoughts can be of bitterness or rebellion, and they exalt themselves against God's truth. In doing so, they become an anti-God thought, an anti-Holy Spirit thought, an anti-Christ thought. A stronghold of spiteful antagonism against your spouse, friend, parent, or whomever can induce headaches, stomach cramps, sleeplessness, and exhaustion. Apart from strongholds being anti-God, we are laying a foundation for hate and divisive action that can end up being a controlling passion in our hearts.

This kind of attitude can attract nervous depression, fear, and weeping because of the wall that has been built up due to our wrong believing. We can be tormented by it. We can wake in the night. We can have dreams of falling, of death, of problems, and the result can be nervous exhaustion. All this is self-inflicted. In a sense, prayer cannot always be the answer because we have to deal with these things by godly sorrow—sorrow in our heart because we have been bitter and antagonistic toward people; we hate them, gossip against them, and are critical of them. Godly sorrow leads to repentance and release. As we forgive ourselves and ask God's forgiveness and forgive the people who maybe we've even imagined have hurt us, liberty can come.

Thoughts seem to have a will of their own. It seems we cannot stop, at times, our thoughts from running wild and conjuring up unreal circumstances that belittle and intimidate others. Those thoughts can systematically destroy us. What is a nervous breakdown but thoughts against ourselves? Self-pity opens a way for all sorts of rejection; we feel that everybody is against us, or doesn't want us, or hurts us. They leave us out. Sometimes this is because we have emanated a force field that repels good words and attracts and accepts negativity into our spirits. As we embrace it, it brings uncontrollable thoughts to power us into subjection.

Paul says to bring your thoughts into captivity before you are at the mercy of uncontrolled malice (see v. 5). Stop your will of wild thinking. Quote verses of Scripture. Demand release from the stranglehold of devilish vengeance and revenge. Make these thoughts bow down to the Lordship of Christ. You cannot let thoughts have mastery of your life, to lord over your emotions, your attitude, or your relationship to others, because that can affect your love for the Lord Jesus. You might become angry with Him. Some people even develop a resentment against God.

I have been absolutely amazed at the number of people who have thoughts against God. They blame God for an accident they've had. Maybe they've lost a loved one, a husband, or wife, or child, or baby. Some situation has gone wrong in their business and they say, "God, why didn't You help us? Haven't I tithed? Haven't I been faithful? Why did You allow this to happen?" And while we may not have said it out loud, we have built up a stronghold against God, against the knowledge of God, against the love of God. By doing that, we distance ourselves from Him and wonder why we're not heard. We may go to church and we just don't enjoy church. It's nothing wrong with church; there's nothing wrong with our prayer. It's the stronghold that holds us captive.

One stronghold can be bitterness. It can affect the way we look, it can change the contour of our face. And bitterness in the Scripture is also interpreted as poison (see Acts 8:23). While we are bitter, it's pumping its deadly venom right through our system. Every cell in our bodies is affected by every thought that we think, so if we have sickness in our bodies, we can have sickness in our minds.

If we believe that we are made for better things, we can achieve better things because good thinking produces good works, which produces, in turn, faith. Faith is a creative power that causes better things to shape the future and to bring the blessing of the Lord into our lives.

We can become hardened in our heart against someone. Maybe they constantly pick on us and find fault with us, always gibing at us, putting a prickle in our spirit because they intimidate us. That can become a stranglehold that controls us—the way we speak, the way we stamp our feet, the way we walk. And we can attract more gibes because a stranglehold of that nature attracts fear and problems. It generates its own atmosphere of frustration and reaction. Competitive, fear-filled thoughts have to be put on the Cross.

Cast down with vigor your argumentative nature. God does not want it in you. It spoils His work He is performing in you, endeavoring to make you like Christ.

Your healthy thinking creates healthy blood cells, blessing, life-giving affirmation, love that's unconditional.

CHAPTER TWENTY-TWO

Don't Believe the Lie

I want to finish up with an area that I feel is important—just to outline again what I feel people need to do to press into their healing. I'm going to entitle this last chapter "Don't Believe the Lie."

Scripture is very clear that woman is under attack from satan in her body. It is evident in Genesis 3, a Scripture passage that we have already looked at.

I believe that the serpent was one of the creatures that had the ability to speak (See Genesis 3:1, 4). We are living in a different age now. The Garden of Eden would have been a perfect generation. I believe that the animals had natures, personalities, and organs of speech. I believe the serpent possibly stood on its legs, and the devil used this beautiful, luminous, possibly fiery serpent, because the devil can change himself into an angel of light. This wasn't any hissing snake; it was a beautiful creature.

I imagine that for some period of time the serpent and all the other animals had conversation and fellowship with Adam and Eve. Adam and God walked among all the creation looking for a help-mate. Although the creatures were beautiful and could converse and had their own personalities, they were not able to have fellowship in a more intimate way with Adam, and so Eve was created. No doubt Adam still had access to all the animals and all the creation, but his greatest fellowship in the cool of the day was with God.

The Lord said that the serpent was subtle, but it was wise and intelligent (see Genesis 3:1). Snakes today are not intelligent. A snake is not the most intelligent of creatures, but no doubt he was before the Fall. Eve was not surprised, nor Adam—did he rush to her aid when he saw the serpent talking with her?—because the serpent talking was a common, matter-of-fact thing, day after day. But no doubt the serpent was walking around seeking how he might devour her. He had another agenda, and no doubt the promise that was given to Adam, all of creation had heard. That's why the serpent had worked out how to answer Eve. This is why the Lord said that the serpent deceived the woman with the intention of destroying her. He felt that she was easier to destroy than Adam.

We can come up with all sorts of conjecture, but let's keep it simple: the serpent is still set to deceive woman and lie to her. He wants to keep her sick. He wants to wreck her body. And while there are natural things that your body has to go through as you get older, satan comes in and takes possession of your blood and your cycles to make you worse.

But God sent His Son to the Cross to die for us that our bodies can be made whole! For the woman with the issue of blood, Jesus came and broke that curse. For the woman who was bowed over He said, "satan has bound you," and He broke satan's bondage. Satan wants to hurt and crush us, but Jesus came to take our crushing and our hurt. We can break the lie of the devil!

You can be better. You can feel better. I would suggest that you take Communion and, in Jesus' Name, break the curse of sickness, break satan's lie on your life. You don't have to be sick. You don't have to have disease. You can be better because the Word of God destroys the works of the enemy—sickness and deception, inferiority, all the complexities of life that have been heightened by his deception. He hates you, but God loves you. Don't listen to the negative, mind-binding spirits that can infest your mind with old ideas, old ways, and old wives' tales. And while many of the things you suffer are real, I'm going to say clearly that the devil did it. He has lied to you. You can be whole. Jesus Christ came to make you whole.

Be whole today, in Jesus' Name. In Jesus' Name, we come against satan's lies. In Jesus' Name, we come against satan's deception. In Jesus' Name, we break the power of the enemy. In Jesus'

Name, we lift off everything satan has put on us. We take out of our minds the concept of sickness, of the curse, of what the devil has put on us. We take it off, and what joy and health satan has taken away, Jesus has come to put back inside of us.

Thank You, Father for health, and life, and blessing, in Jesus' Name. You've taken our pain and our sorrow. These are not part of our lives, in Jesus' Name. Release us now, in Jesus' Name. Release us from the power of the curse of sin, from the power of sickness, from the deceiver's grip. Jesus Christ is the Lord of our lives. We thank Him for our wellbeing. We thank Him for our prosperity, for our freedom, for our liberty in God.

You have to break off the concept that you can't change. You *can* change. You *can* get better. You don't have to stay the way you are. The power of Jesus' Name has come to break the lie of satan. Jesus said, "I am the truth and I am the way" (see John 14:6). God has truth, which is to heal you. He is the way of life. He has come to give it to you abundantly so your whole personality can change, your financial structure can change, and also your relationship with Him. He is a loving, beautiful, heavenly Father. He has a glorious Son, the Lord Jesus Christ, and the Holy Spirit—the Comforter—is here to help us in all our ways, to reveal the Word of God to us, to reveal the Father, to reveal our relationships. We don't have to be pushy, matriarchal, or domineering. We don't have to have adverse sexual drives. We can be normal in every way. Jesus came to make us normal. Christianity is a beautiful thing. Jesus Christ came to bless you and set you free.

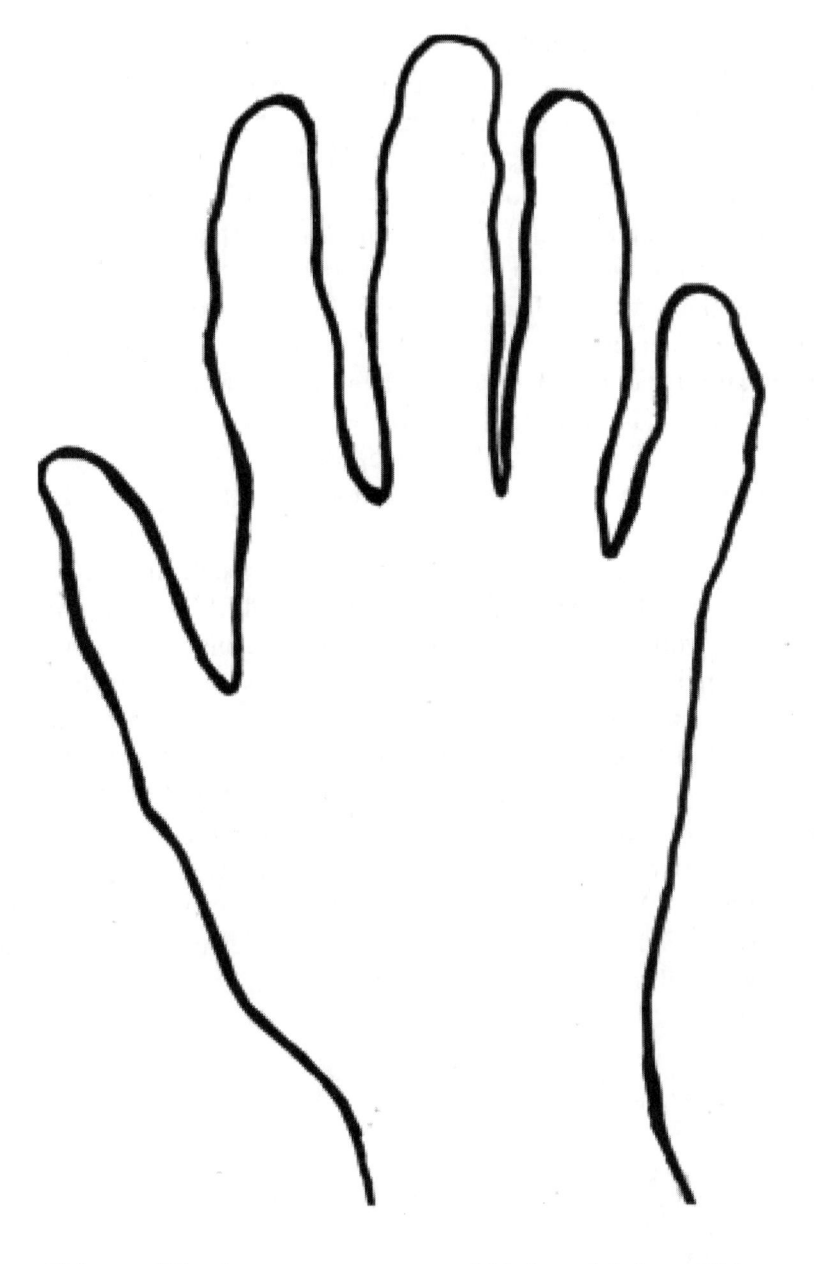

"They will take up serpents; and if they drink anything deadly, it will by no means hurt them; they will lay hands on the sick, and they will recover."

Mark 16:18